What people are saying about

A Walk on the Wild Side

"There is no experience like first-hand experience", says Gary Williams, "and I have had many of them." In this lively and enjoyable book he shares many of them with the reader, whether they were positive, like his sittings with mediums Brian Hurst, Warren Smith, Albert Best and Alex Tanous and an encounter with a poltergeist, or negative, as in the case of a well-known couple who he describes as "blatant frauds". He also has little time for fashionable TV "mediums" who somehow manage to keep going despite evidence of their fakery. I would advise any of these pretenders who come across Gary to run away and hide.

Good travel guides know their chosen areas. In this book, readers are in safe hands as they are guided through several of those mysterious regions often lumped together and labelled "paranormal"- from UFOs, ghosts and EVPs, (electronic voice phenomena), to precognitive dreams, predictions and reincarnation. Homage is also paid to such members of the Hall of Fame psychical research as Leslie Flint, Edgar Cayce, and especially the author's friend Alex Tanous. There are also chapters on astrology, which Gary practises, and religion, about which he has his reservations.

The book is as informative as it is enjoyable reading, and its author comes across as an honest seeker of truth who does his best to clarify an often misunderstood subject.

Guy Lyon Playfair

T0302945

A Walk on the Wild Side

One Man's Experiences with Psychic Phenomena

A Walk on the Wild Side

One Man's Experiences with Psychic Phenomena

Gary Williams

With an Introduction by Guy Playfair

BOOKS

Winchester, UK
Washington, USA

First published by Sixth Books, 2018
Sixth Books is an imprint of John Hunt Publishing Ltd., No. 3 East Street,
Alresford, Hampshire SO24 9EE, UK
office1@jhpbooks.net
www.johnhuntpublishing.com
www.6th-books.com

For distributor details and how to order please visit the 'Ordering' section on our website.

ISBN: 978 1 78535 776 3
978 1 78535 777 0 (ebook)
Library of Congress Control Number: 2017943754

A CIP catalogue record for this book is available from the British Library.

Design: Stuart Davies

Printed and bound by CPI Group (UK) Ltd, Croydon, CR0 4YY, UK

We operate a distinctive and ethical publishing philosophy in
all areas of our business, from our global network of authors to
production and worldwide distribution.

Contents

For my father Wallace Gordon Williams
And for Alex Tanous

Introduction

by Guy Lyon Playfair

"There is no experience like first-hand experience," says Gary Williams, "and I have had many of them." In this lively and enjoyable book he shares many of them with the reader, whether they were positive, like his sittings with mediums Brian Hurst, Warren Smith, Albert Best and Alex Tanous and an encounter with a poltergeist, or negative, as in the case of a well-known couple who he describes as "blatant frauds". He also has little time for fashionable TV "mediums" who somehow manage to keep going despite evidence of their fakery. I would advise any of these pretenders who come across Gary to run away and hide.

Good travel guides know their chosen areas. In this book, readers are in safe hands as they are guided through several of those mysterious regions often lumped together and labelled "paranormal", from UFOs, ghosts and EVPs, (electronic voice phenomena), to precognitive dreams, predictions and reincarnation. Homage is paid to such members of the Hall of Fame psychical research as Leslie Flint, Edgar Cayce, and especially the author's friend Alex Tanous. There are also chapters on astrology, which Gary practises, and religion, about which he has his reservations.

The book is as informative as it is enjoyable reading, and its author comes across as an honest seeker of truth who does his best to clarify an often misunderstood subject.

Guy Lyon Playfair
London, England
20 February, 2016

Preface

A writer needs a pretty good reason to introduce yet another book on the paranormal into today's crowded market. Though there are many books about psychic subjects, and not a few about ghosts and hauntings not to mention a popular TV show in which amateur ghost hunters (who are really plumbers) try their best to discern some kind of haunting phenomenon where there may not be any; there are precious few books about psychic phenomena that force us to look at the world through a different lens. For if any of the things I say in this book are true then we must establish a new world view. New paradigms must be constructed that allow for the continuity of consciousness after physical death. This should not be too difficult because quantum physics is now establishing that there may be multiple dimensions beyond the physical one. My experiences with psychic phenomena point to the idea that there are indeed such dimensions.

My friends say I am secretive and devious. That such an individual should undertake a work of autobiography, albeit optimistically impersonal, must seem at least perverse and at best brazen. But therein may dwell a certain stimulus to titillation, if not to honourable intellectual exertion. The secretive person, you see, supposes himself on terms of such private and artful intimacy with the truth that he can thread his way without deceit but also without inexpedient disclosure through the narration of a story which is his own only to the extent that it reveals him utterly and honestly. This, of course, is the beauty of his predicament, and it may make for a certain aesthetic effect, setting the matter of contemplation apart from the means of its comprehension. Writers are regarded as privileged eccentrics.

In writing this book I felt it was time to take a fresh look at such subjects as ghosts, hauntings, poltergeists, flying saucers, out of body experiences, near death experiences and the prediction of the future, and probably more important than any of the others: the meaning of life.

My psychic journey began while I was a teenager in high school; while at the library I stumbled upon a book entitled *The World of Psychic Phenomena* by Florence S. Edsall. The book opened up a whole new world for me full of things to explore which were unexplained. I had no idea at that time that it would launch me on a journey that would last me the rest of my life. I have had enough "proof" to convince me of the reality of psychic phenomena but beyond that I believe I have been fortunate enough to grasp the meaning of these experiences beyond what they appear to be on the surface.

The communications from my father after his death have convinced me of the reality of life after death. When I wrote *A Life Beyond Death* in 1989 science was just on the cutting edge exploring the idea of multiple dimensions. Now it seems a comfortable fit for "where we go when we die". We cannot visualize another world ruled by quite other laws, the reason being that we live in a specific world which has helped to shape our minds and establish our basic psychic conditions. However, there are indications that at least part of the psyche is not subject to the laws of space and time. Scientific proof of that has been provided by the well-known researcher J. B. Rhine in Durham, North Carolina at Duke University. Along with numerous cases of spontaneous foreknowledge, non-spatial perceptions, and so on – of which I have had numerous experiences in my own life – these experiments prove that the psyche at times functions outside of space and time, and therefore of causality also. This indicates that our conceptions of space and time are incomplete. A complete picture of the world would require the addition of still another dimension; only then could the totality of phenomena be given a unified explanation. Hence it is that the rationalists insist to this day that parapsychological experiences do not really exist; for their world-view stands or falls by this question. If such phenomena occur at all, the rationalistic picture of the universe is invalid, because it is incomplete. Then the possibility of an other-valued reality behind the phenomenal world becomes an inescapable problem, and we must face the fact that our world, with its time, space, and causality, relates to another order of things lying behind or beneath it, in which neither "here and there" nor "earlier and later" are of importance. Grasping these concepts, albeit abstract and uncomfortable, will help us to understand the possibility of life after death. If there were no life after death there would be no point in this life either. It would indeed be a shallow, meaningless existence.

The subjects I am going to explore in this book are out of the ordinary. At moments it may seem as if I am asking you to believe in "six impossible things before breakfast". But thankfully science is moving on. What would have been considered impossible one hundred years ago is commonplace today. One hundred years ago planes could not fly and as one scientist exclaimed, "I have examined Mr Edison's invention and it is nothing but sheer trickery." He was speaking of the phonograph. There were no meteorites because as Lavoiser said, "Everyone knows there are no stones in the sky."

Great strides have been made in other new areas too. As physicist and UFO researcher Stanton Friedman says, "New discoveries in science are made by doing something different in an unconventional way." When first invented who would have thought that the tape recorder would be used as a means to communicate with the dead. And yet Electronic Voice Phenomena have been established beyond any reasonable doubt and it is something any person can do on a home tape recorder.

Cracks are starting to appear in many formerly held scientific dogmas. It is becoming clear that the mind and the brain are not the same thing. This is difficult for some people to grasp inasmuch as most human beings are very tied up with their concepts of the physical body being the be-all and end-all of existence. But as psychologist William James said, "There is no pain in the world like the pain of a new idea." The flying saucer phenomena which were once a subject of ridicule is now being forced to be taken seriously as governments other than the USA are coming forward with evidence that cannot be refuted. Whistle-blowers have admitted that they were forced to lie or participate in a cover-up concerning alien beings or crashed saucers.

The seeds that were planted 125 years ago with the founding of the Society for Psychical Research are just now beginning to bear fruit and open the door wide to proof of survival of death. The Leslie Flint direct voice recordings, of which there are thousands, are now on YouTube for everyone to listen to, bearing firsthand evidence of what happens to people when they die. Parapsychology holds it to be a scientifically valid proof of an afterlife when the dead manifest themselves – either as ghosts, or through a medium – and communicate things which they alone could possibly know. Still, there is doubt which can only be removed by further experimentation.

This book is designed for young people of all ages, by which I mean those whose imagination has not been stifled by the standard educational process. It is written for people who can still be awed by the way ants build their burrows, by the cold elegance of a snake, or the beauty of a flower. I am writing for people who can tolerate a temporary state of ambiguity, for those who can take change easily and are not afraid of handling wild ideas. Those who cannot tolerate change will drop out very quickly. Few scientists will read this book to the end. But I do hope that it will stimulate the thinking processes and implant some ideas into the minds of future scientists.

In this book, I am attempting to build a model of the universe that will satisfy the need for a comprehensive picture of "what our existence is all about". In other words, a holistic model that encompasses not only the physical, observable universe that is our immediate environment and the distant universe observed by astronomers but also other realities as well. Most of us see the universe through a tiny window, which allows us to see just a single colour, or reality, out of the endless spectrum of realities. Viewing our universe through this tiny window forces us to see the world in a sequential form, that is, as events that follow each other in time. This is not necessarily so.

Little did I know that the book I read in the library fifty years ago would take me on a journey that would lead to experiences which few people, if any, have had. It has truly been a "walk on the wild side".

Gary Williams
Marbella, Spain
4 May 2015

Chapter One

Carl Jung Opens the Door to the Psychic

What I have to tell about the hereafter, and about life after death, consists entirely of memories, of images in which I have lived and of the thoughts which have buffeted me. These memories in a way also underlie my works; for the latter are fundamentally nothing but attempts ever renewed, to give an answer to the question of the interplay between the "here" and the "hereafter". Yet I have never written expressly about a life after death; for then I would have had to document my ideas, and I have no way of doing that. Be that as it may, I would like to state my ideas now.
Carl Jung, *Memories, Dreams, Reflections*

I started out as a child. I came from a middle class southern Mason Dixon line Virginia family. My father was a newspaper advertising executive, my mother was a housewife. But underneath that veneer was the desire to break out all the time. My childhood was not filled with provocative psychic experiences. In fact, it wasn't until high school that a milestone occurred in my life that became so memorable I have carried it with me all my life. My high school biology teacher, Elba Hubbard and her husband John started taking the class on a series of field trips. The purpose, no doubt, was to broaden our view of life. Our first field trip was to the zoo. I was particularly enchanted with the giraffes. With their long necks they seemed to be able to see further than any of us and for that reason I admired them.

Our second field trip was to a Spiritualist Church. For the unenlightened, Spiritualism is a religion founded on the principles that there is no death and that the dead can communicate with the living. The church was a modest frame building in an unassuming section of Norfolk, Virginia, the city in which I was born. The service we attended on a Sunday night consisted of the singing of some hymns, the reading of some Bible passages and a short sermon. Then the medium stood up and began delivering messages to people in the audience which we were assured came from our loved ones in the Spirit World. She went from one to another, passing messages to this person and that person until she finally came to me.

"I have a man here," she said, "who died of cancer and he tells me he is your uncle." My uncle, Lud Garthe, my father's sister's husband had indeed died of cancer the previous year. "He assures me that this is the first of many contacts and that you will go on to explore this subject with a much wider vision." The evidential bit was that I only had one uncle and he had indeed died of cancer. The second part I could not validate but it indeed proved to be true considering I have spent the rest of my life investigating this subject.

Then, as we were going out the door of the church, we noticed a blackboard on which was written a notice. "Materialisation séance next Friday". "Medium is Warren Smith". Mrs Hubbard immediately signed us up. I had no idea what I was in for but as we were filling in the form a rather stout lad approached us and told us that we first must have attended a trumpet séance before we could attend the materialisation séance. I had no idea what a trumpet séance was and for that matter no idea what a materialisation séance was either. I later discovered that both were forms of something called physical mediumship in which a substance called ectoplasm is drawn from the medium while in a trance. This ectoplasm is then moulded into the form of a deceased loved one in the case of materialisation, or into a replica of the human voice box in the case of the trumpet séance, the trumpet being a cylindrical cone which is said to help amplify the sound.

At this point I should point out the fact that physical mediumship was rife with fraud and for this reason there are hardly any physical mediums around today. Leslie Flint, who I will speak of in a later chapter, was the last genuine direct voice medium. He died in 1994. The reason for so much fraud is simply that this type of mediumship usually takes place in darkness or in a red light, white light supposedly harming the mediumistic process.

In the first two decades of legitimate psychical research scandals involving physical mediumship were legion. The number of frauds in the field produced the unfortunate effect of suggesting that scientists who looked upon any form of psychic phenomena as genuine were indulging in wishful thinking.

In the latter part of the nineteenth century debunkers had a field-day exposing the Fox sisters in America who had produced raps by cracking their toes, and the Italian medium Eusapia Palladini in Britain who fooled no one. In her presence guitars played by themselves, bells rang and lights would appear. Her cheating was so clumsy that all but the most ardent Spiritualists denounced her. Even the notorious Douglas Home was called up and accused on more than one occasion of producing fraudulent phenomena. Home was supposed to have floated out of a second-storey building in London in the presence of witnesses, one of whom was Lord Adare. Later debunkers accused Home of having homosexual relations with Adare.

Then in 1880, Florence Cook was caught impersonating a spirit she called "Marie". In the presence of not-so-clever sitters in the séance room, "Marie" walked around, seemingly lifelike in every respect. Too lifelike, in fact, for when she passed by the chair of Sir George Sitwell, father of Edith, he grabbed her and held on tight until someone could turn on the light. Then it was discovered that "Marie" was Florence Cook in her underwear. Similarly, in 1873, a man by the name of Volkman had grabbed Florence while she was pretending to materialise a figure who she called "Katie King". Years later, through the influence of William Crookes, the discoverer of thallium, Florence was cleared. But the damage had been done. These preposterous scandals had the unfortunate effect of spreading the impression that most mediums were such frauds that no sane person would waste time on them.

However, on that Friday night in October 1966 I was unaware of any of these things and all I had to go on was what I was told. Namely that the medium would go into a trance and materialised spirits would appear. The room in which we sat was in fact brilliantly lit in a strong red light, so much so that it was possible to see everyone sitting in the room including their facial features. We sat in a circle around the room and I would estimate that there were about twenty people present. After a while the medium, Warren Smith, entered the room. He told us his name and then went straight to the far end of the room and sat in a chair behind some curtains which I later learned was called the cabinet. Then a woman came up and stood before us and gave some instructions. She said we were never to touch the materialisations unless permission was given to do so. Touching the materialisations was about the last thing I wanted to do, in fact getting out of the room was foremost on my mind. I was actually sitting in front of the only door in the room, the only way in and the only way out. I need also mention that the floor was solid concrete. There were no concealed trap doors in the floor as some debunkers have suggested years later. Fraud seemed impossible.

After a while we were told to sing. The explanation for this was that singing created power to build the ectoplasmic figures. And so we sang. The song we sang was "East side, West side, all the around the town, the sidewalks of New York". We sang this song over and over for about twenty minutes until I began to see a smoky substance pour out from behind the curtain where the medium was sitting. This substance slowly but surely built up into the solid form of a woman. To avoid any possibility of misinterpretation let me emphatically state that this woman did not walk out from behind the curtains. There is no way it could have been rigged. And I was sitting in front of the only door. When the figure became totally solid the woman announced that her name was Firefly and that she was the medium's Guide. The next thing she did was pull back the curtains to show us that the medium, Warren Smith, was slumped over in his chair, apparently asleep. She then proceeded to walk around the room and speak to every one of us saying she would do her best to try and bring our loved ones in Spirit. At that point I started thinking that there really wasn't anyone who was dead who I wanted to see. Fifty years later it becomes clear that there is nothing frightening about speaking with someone who is deceased. The spookiness has derived from Hollywood movies where people sit around a table holding hands and someone muttering in a trance. This scenario was portrayed in the film *Séance On a Wet Afternoon*. My experience was nothing like this. As a matter of fact my experiences with psychic phenomena of all kinds over the years runs counter to what most people believe is true or would like to believe because they have done no research of their own on the subject and have had no first-hand experiences. But at sixteen years of age all I could think about was getting out of that room. This séance lasted well over three hours. During that time I saw little children materialise solid and run up to their parents who were sitting in the circle. Facial features were easily distinguishable. The most astonishing thing about this exhibition was the way that the materialised figures went away. They literally sank down and disappeared into the cement floor. This was an impossibility but it happened. Perhaps because of my age or perhaps because of the strangeness of the situation I was visibly frightened throughout the entire proceedings. In fact, I was so frightened that I had my eyes closed. I was dreading the moment when my turn would come and it finally came!

The cabinet attendant lady (the woman who was telling me all along not to be frightened) called me to the middle of the room. I stood in the middle of the room and waited and in about a minute my uncle, Lud Garthe, was standing there just as real as in life. This was too much. I nearly fainted dead away! I began a hasty retreat back to my chair. And he, like all the others, disappeared right down into the cement floor. But there was "more to come", only this wasn't the *Tonight Show* with Johnny Carson. I no sooner got back to my seat when I was called back and told that there was another person, a man who had only recently passed away who wanted to come and speak to me and this was a very important person. It was the medium's Guide, Firefly, who told me this. Once again the smoky substance started to build up. Within minutes I recognized the features of a man who looked to be about seventy-five years old. The man came forward and took my hand and shook it. Then he said, "My name is Carl Jung. I am in your band." What was this supposed to mean? "I am in your band". What kind of band? "I am one of your guides," he explained. "Each and every person on the earth has a guide or two and I am in your band of guides and helpers. Let me assure you that when you are older you will delve deeply into these mysteries of life and death and make many discoveries on your own. For now just know that I am around you." I was dazed. I still found it hard to believe that this man was standing solid in front of me. So I took a piece of Wrigley's chewing gum out of my coat pocket and handed it to him saying, "If you're real, take this and crumple it up and hand it back to me," which he did. I had that stick of chewing gum for three years. I had no idea who Carl Jung was. I had never heard of him. But when I went to school on Monday I went and got a book out of the library and saw his picture and it was that man! There is no way it could have been faked. Little did I know at the time of the Warren Smith séance that Carl Jung was deeply interested in life after death during his earth life and in fact was a Spiritualist so it is deeply convincing that he would associate himself with this subject. Carl Jung's doctoral dissertation was not medical research but the investigation of a medium, Helene Preiswerk. His mother, Emile was born into a family that regularly practised Spiritualism, the daughter of a man who held weekly séances with his dead first wife who instructed young Emile to stand behind his chair to discourage ghosts. Jung showed a willingness to take Spiritualism seriously at this formative stage in his life and the early experiences with Helene Preiswerk suggest a credence of Spiritualism as possible evidence of the supernatural. The last chapter of his autobiography, *Memories, Dreams, Reflections* is entitled, "Life After Death".

Freud and Jung were probably the most famous psychologists in history, so why me? This I cannot answer. I know it happened. I was there. On our way home from the séance my teacher tried her best to convince me that it was mass hallucination. She could not bring herself to believe in an afterlife. I felt sorry for her and still do to this day even though she and her husband are both long dead. Years later, when I was in my twenties, I went out to their house and discussed the incident. "Why would Carl Jung come to see you?" she asked. She believed that the only messages about life after death were the messages in the Bible and there was no point in looking further. My teacher was like the attitude of the SETI organization which ufologist Stanton Friedman calls Silly Effort to Investigate. The letters actually stand for Search for Extraterrestrial Intelligence but I like Silly Effort to Investigate better. The organization is using radio telescopes to listen for messages from outer space. But as Stan points out the problem is that the aliens are already here so why would they be sending out messages? And why would they be using outdated technology such as radio signals? Just like my teacher who believed that any current evidence was impossible and that only information which was received two thousand years ago is valid. But as Stanton Friedman has pointed out one can only draw serious conclusions by doing research on your own.

People who have done no research or only armchair research are not entitled to an opinion Friedman says. And I agree.

How can we get past the bias that if a person accepts these kinds of phenomena as valid he is also likely to believe in "six impossible things before breakfast" as Lewis Carroll writes in *Alice Through the Looking Glass*? I see nothing wrong with healthy scepticism. But there is a difference between being a sceptic and being a debunker. The debunker has such a bias against the subject that even in the face of undeniable evidence he would not admit to its truth. I do not believe that a sceptical attitude contributes in any way to blocking or inhibiting psychic phenomena. A particularly good example of this is found in the case of Sir Osbert Sitwell. Sitwell's father was a well-known sceptic, and one of his escapades in "unmasking a medium" illustrates the point. His son tells how, just before the First World War, he and some brother officers went to see a famous palmist in London. The woman looked at their hands, and was obviously deeply disturbed. Sitwell went back to her when the others had gone, and asked her what the matter was. She told him: "I could see *nothing* in their hands." A few months later, the war started, and these officers were dead.

I visited other Spiritualist churches following the Warren Smith séance but I never again was able to attend a materialisation séance. This kind of mediumship had declined drastically by the end of the 1960s. Probably the most famous materialisation medium was Ethel Post Parrish who held court at a Spiritualist camp called Camp Silver Belle. She became an extremely prominent American physical medium. Her phases of direct voice and materialisation attracted world-wide attention. In 1927 Ethel Post Parrish opened a church and established a school for Spiritualist ministers and the development of mediums in Miami, Florida. To escape the intense heat and humidity of Florida's summers, in 1932 she opened a summer camp and school for mediumship in Ephrata, Pennsylvania. She named it Camp Silver Belle after her Indian guide. During her life she submitted to numerous tests to prove the truth of her mediumship. A series of infra-red photographs were taken at 50-second intervals of one of her séances which was witnessed by eighty-one people.

Another extremely well documented materialisation medium was Alec Harris from Wales. Harris moved to South Africa where he conducted the bulk of his séances and readings. Harris was known for his ability to materialise more than one figure at a time which many believed ruled out fraud. Spirit forms showed themselves in good red light and held sustained conversations, after having walked about ten feet from the cabinet. At one séance, thirty forms materialised during a two and a half hour séance. Harris never charged for his services, deriving his income from government work. A sitter named Alec Hewitt attended one of Harris's séances. He hung his overcoat in the hall and came into the room. The door was locked and a table was placed against it to reassure Alec Hewitt that nobody could enter. As soon as the light was extinguished something was dropped into Mr. Hewitt's lap. When the lights were eventually put on he found his keys in his lap. He was puzzled because he had left them in the pocket of his overcoat in the hall. Yet, there they were, transported through the locked and barricaded door. This left him with much to think about and no physical explanation to account for it.

Helen Duncan was another famous materialisation medium. She practised in the 1930s and 1940s. She was tried under the Witchcraft Act and sent to prison. She used paper mache dolls suspended from coat hangers.

Following the Warren Smith séance in 1966 I was off seeking new psychic adventures. The name of Edgar Cayce loomed large in my search. Cayce (pronounced Kay-see) was an American psychic who possessed the ability to answer questions on subjects as varied as healing, reincarnation, wars, Atlantis and future events while in a trance. These answers came to be known as "life readings" and were delivered to individuals while Cayce was hypnotized. This ability gave him the nickname "The Sleeping Prophet". Cayce founded a non-profit organization, the Association for Research and Enlightenment at 67th and Atlantic avenues in Virginia Beach, Virginia, less than twenty miles from where I was born. Cayce became a celebrity toward the end of his life. He believed that the publicity given to his prophecies overshadowed the more important parts of his work such as healing.

The original "life readings" of Edgar Cayce are preserved in a modern looking building that faces the ocean in Virginia Beach. I must have been about eighteen when I first went there, as I recall very well, I was told by my ex-biology teacher who I named "debunker Hubbard" that this was one I shouldn't miss. I remember it vividly because it was the same month that I started a new job as a classical radio presenter on a radio station in Norfolk where the building turned out to be haunted. The day I went to the A.R.E it was a hot, humid August day in Virginia. Virginia Beach draws crowds of people in the summer. Half had come to be on the beach and the other half to visit the Edgar Cayce library. Everything is on file cards by subject heading. For example, if you wanted to know what Cayce had said about Atlantis you would find every reading that he ever gave that mentioned the subject. Cayce predicted that the ruins of Atlantis would be discovered in 1969. In that year, off the coast of Florida, the "Bimini Road" was discovered which many believe is part of the ruins of Atlantis. It is a series of stones which appear to be in the shape of a road and made by human hands.

While his predictions were startling, Cayce's greatest contribution was in the readings which he gave to people to help them get well. Cayce had no medical training and remembered nothing when he came out of trance. The most amazing part, however, was that the person for whom he was giving the reading was usually not even present at the time it was given and, in fact, could be thousands of miles away. The only thing that Cayce required was the name of the person he was giving the reading for and the location of where that person was at that precise moment. After this information was given to him Cayce would pause for a moment and then say, "Yes, we have the body here," and then go on to make some remark about what the person was doing at the time or some particular item of clothing that they happened to be wearing. Cayce's medical advice was unorthodox and it wasn't until after scores of people reported getting well that he began to take his own readings seriously. Cayce was devoutly religious, taught Sunday School to the end of his life and rejected many of the things that came through his own readings like reincarnation and comments about religion in general. I found the Cayce readings fascinating and returned again and again throughout the years to the A.R.E. It was in the library there that I met writer Jess Stearn, the author of *Edgar Cayce: The Sleeping Prophet*. Jess introduced me to actress Susan Strasberg. Susan's father was Lee Strasberg who had found the Method Acting School in New York where Marilyn Monroe studied. Years later, over lunch in Los Angeles, Susan told me how she was certain that Marilyn was murdered, having received psychic communications from her. It was in that same library in Virginia Beach, that I did the bulk of my research for my book *A Life Beyond Death*. Toward the end of her life I brought my mother to the A.R.E to try to find a cure for her breathing disorder which had resulted from breathing in years of my father's second-hand smoke. Psychic and healer Alex Tanous also had a try but it was too late.

Clairvoyants like Cayce, Nostradamus, and other names that loom large upon the scene are the well-known ones. But there have been others too. Gerard Croiset, a Dutch psychic, probably contributed more to psychical research in the way of precognition tests than anyone. Croiset would be told to pick a chair in a lecture hall where a lecture would be given weeks later. He would then describe the person who would come to sit in that chair. Hundreds of these tests were made and Croiset scored high; more about him in a later chapter. The late Joseph DeLouise of Chicago made his living predicting the Chicago stock market. When I went to see him in 1989 he lay down on the floor and went into a trance.

The days of the great mediums such as Douglas Home, Eusapia Palladino, Leonore Piper seemed to be at an end by the time of the Second World War. There were still many remarkable mediums, Mrs. Osborne Leonard, Rudi Schneider, but their achievements were not all that spectacular. In the cynical and disillusioned frame of mind of the time, exposures and denunciations received far more publicity than successful experiments with mediums. After a series of experiments with the Austrian medium Rudi Schneider, investigator Harry Price denounced him in a Sunday newspaper instead of simply making an unfavourable report to the Society for Psychical Research. And when Helen Duncan was charged with cheating and fined ten pounds, Price wrote a book attacking her. In due course, Price himself would be denounced for trickery in his most famous investigation, the haunting of Borley Rectory.

Writer Colin Wilson tells the story of his invitation to attend a materialisation séance at the home of medium Rita Goold in the 1980s. I first heard about Rita Goold from trance medium Ray Smith in Gibraltar while I was writing *A Life Beyond Death*. She was purported to be able to materialise spirits in solid form, the same as Warren Smith and Ethel Post Parrish. When I telephoned Goold I asked her if she had been tested. "But this has all been done", Goold retorted, "I have even been to the Palace." When I asked her what palace, she replied Buckingham Palace. I told her as interesting as that might be, witnessing one of her sittings wearing night vision goggles would make more of an impression on me. At this point she put down the phone.

I have always agreed with the philosophy of the late Alex Tanous who insisted that mediums, psychics and clairvoyants submit to stringent tests. Alex himself was tested in hundreds of out-of-body trials at the American Society for Psychical Research in New York. As far as I know Rita Goold was never formally tested in a laboratory although Professor Archie Roy and Tony Cornell, both members of the Society for Psychical Research attended one of her séances and came away with mixed feelings. Colin Wilson had no mixed feelings, however, in recalling his sitting with Rita Goold. Unlike my experience in 1966 with medium Warren Smith that took place in strong red light, Goold worked in total darkness:

> I asked "Helen Duncan", one of the purported spirits, if she could explain the nature of poltergeists. "I will explain," said "Helen" magisterially. But she did not explain. Instead she told us that poltergeists had never harmed anyone, and that there was no need to be afraid of them. For the next quarter of an hour she rambled on, saying nothing in particular, certainly nothing about the nature of poltergeists. It became clear that either she knew nothing about poltergeists, or preferred to keep it to herself.
>
> I was told that Sir Oliver Lodge's son Raymond usually appeared at their séances so I asked whether I might meet him. Eventually, after more conversation, Raymond arrived, and introduced himself to me. It was at this point that my vague doubts began to become insistent. This "Raymond" spoke in a rather slow voice, with an upper-class accent, and a slightly feminine intonation, like Ella Sheilds as "Burlington Bertie".
>
> I asked him if it was true that spirits could see in the dark, and he confirmed this. So I asked if he could tell me what expression I was wearing on my face at the moment. I pulled a horribly distorted face and thrust out my lips. "You

mean if you've got your mouth open or something?" And quite suddenly, I knew beyond all doubt that "Raymond" could not see in the dark. I said yes, that was what I meant. "Raymond" replied promptly that he didn't do that anymore. Why not? I asked, and he explained that it convinced no one. "But it would convince me," I told him. "For example, if you could tell me how many fingers I am now holding up." I held up two fingers. If he could tell me how many fingers I was holding up, I would accept that he was a spirit. If not, I wouldn't. He couldn't.

But there was none of this fakery in the Warren Smith séance which I attended as a teenager. It was not held in the dark, and I could see everyone in the room including the medium in the cabinet. It was impossible for the medium to be parading around pretending to be a materialised spirit. I am reminded of Alexander Hero, the fictitious investigator from the Society for Psychical Research in Paul Gallico's novel, *The Hand of Mary Constable*. Hero attends a materialisation séance in which the deceased daughter of a prominent scientist is supposed to be able to materialise. The young girl asks "Daddy" to give her some secret information that he is working on for the government. Hero suspects that the proceedings are fake. Using the alias of Peter Fairweather, Hero attends a séance in which the medium, Mrs Bessmer, asks to be tied up, supposedly to avoid fraud. Gallico writes in *The Hand of Mary Constable*:

The assistant rose and went to the cabinet with Mrs Bessmer, where, from behind one of the curtains she produced a length of heavy clothesline cord, some twenty feet of it. Mrs Bessmer sat in the chair by the table, and little Woodmanston bound her to it by the legs, arms, and chest, winding and rewinding the rope about her lumpy figure, stopping only to fashion an intricate knot, then continuing until the last foot of cord was exhausted and she was trussed up like a mummy. He returned to his chair next to Peter Fairweather, glowing with satisfaction and pride. "There," he said. "No doubts, eh?"

Alexander Hero chortled within himself and thought: *Thirty seconds and you'll be out of there. If I tied you, Mother dear, you would never budge in a month of Sundays.* Hero, of course, would have used a spool of thread, that anathema of the fake medium. For with the bit of strain applied, or struggle to evade, the thread would snap and with it the proof. No mediums Hero had ever known would permit themselves to be bound by the wrists or thumbs with ordinary sewing cotton.

I had a similar experience to Colin Wilson's when I attended a series of direct voice séances in Doncaster in 1988 with the medium Sandy Meakin Jones just prior to the publication of my book *A Life Beyond Death*. The publishers were interested in my bringing out another book right away, and the subject I was most interested in at the time was a type of physical mediumship called direct voice, or more accurately, independent direct voice. In this type of mediumship the lifelike voice of the spirit communicator is heard in mid-space about five feet from the medium's head. The actual physical larynx of the medium is not used. Probably the most famous of the direct voice mediums was Leslie Flint who died in 1994. But by the time my book had come out Flint had retired. I wrote to him several times and had no reply. It became obvious that door was closed.

It was at about this time that I read a series of articles in *Psychic News* about a new medium who possessed the rare gift of direct voice. Her name was Sandy Meakin Jones. I wrote to her asking for tapes of her séances. She sent them in due course and the voices sounded convincing. One of the communicators was said to be Charles de Gaulle. This worried me because whenever famous people appear there is always the doubt of fraud. Sandy told me she was not practising her mediumship for money and invited me to come to England and attend a series of séances.

As in the case of any type of physical phenomena, it is necessary to be present in order to make a valid judgement. I recalled the reluctance of the Society for Psychical Research to dispatch investigators to Brazil in 1890 to investigate Carlos Mirabelli who was said to levitate in the presence of reliable witnesses and to be able to produce materialised figures in broad daylight. The obvious step would have been for psychical researchers to undertake an investigation, but they were otherwise occupied (with the investigation of Mina Crandon, a Boston medium) and had no funds for such an enterprise. Nothing was done.

I went to England and met the medium in August 1988 and held fourteen séances with her. The séances were held in total darkness, the voices produced through an ectoplasmic voice box which is extraneous from the medium. The medium did not go into trance. I witnessed numerous conversations between the medium and the communicators.

The medium was then forty-five years old. She told me that she had exhibited psychic gifts from the age of two and she discovered that she could see and hear people whom others could not

"I was discouraged from talking about it," she told me, "and I always kept it to myself. Somehow, though, I knew there would be a turning point in my life where this would come into focus."

The turning point came in 1980, following the death of her husband. After visiting a medium who told her to go to a Spiritualist church, she attended an open circle in 1982. "I was told by a lovely old lady there, Mary Hughes, that I had this ability."

Unable to locate either a medium or a development circle with whom she felt comfortable, Sandy began to sit alone for development and succeeded in demonstrating a considerable amount of clairvoyant and clairaudient ability. In 1985, while meditating, she began to receive the information about a room with nothing in it but two chairs. On the appointed day Sandy and I drove to York and we sat in the blacked-out room. I played no music. Within minutes of switching off the light a deep masculine voice was heard in the centre of the room which soon identified itself as Black Cloud, one of the medium's guides. At this point I covered Sandy's mouth with my hand. The voice kept on speaking. So at this point I knew that a paranormal voice, totally independent from the medium, was speaking in mid-space in my blacked-out bedroom. The next question would be "Who was speaking?"

I put off arranging my editor from Hale to visit the Doncaster circle until I was able to have one or two more sittings in Sandy's circle to question the communicators about a number of points. It was fortunate for me that I did this because the nature of the information which was coming through seemed so odd that I began to question if perhaps the communicators were frauds.

On the occasion of the next circle "Charles de Gaulle" spoke to me for almost half an hour explaining how "they" would have to act if certain things in our world did not change very soon. "We will leave no stone unturned," he said. "If it takes all of the medium's lifetime, we will be heard. If conditions do not change, are not altered, we will be forced to act. You will see strange lights in the sky which will be blue. These are to be a sign to you that many changes are to take place in your world as you know it." To accept this belief would mean that the spirit world would chastise or punish people of the earth in some way which, to me, sounded absurd. Then there were the communications purporting to come from my father who died in 1984. It was definitely my father's voice but the things he said made no sense. I asked him, "What do you think of the changes at home?" My mother had recently met a man and remarried. The man was not to my liking and he felt likewise. My "father" replied it seems you are doing very well." When I explained that it was my mother who I was referring to, he became confused and left. Like Colin Wilson, I felt that something was seriously wrong. I rang my editor and told her not to come. I made preparations to return to California. I thanked the medium and took my leave quickly, anxious to avoid further embarrassment.

It was not until my return to California and a meeting with Hollywood medium Brian Hurst that things began to become clear. Brian had written the foreword to *A Life Beyond Death*. Born and raised in the UK, Brian came to California to escape the British weather. By the time the book was out I had had several sittings with him. Brian is a mental medium, meaning he receives impressions and must interpret them and pass them on to the sitter. Although he was also a trance medium (a condition in which he goes to sleep and a spirit person controls his speech), Brian never used trance in his sittings with the general public. His guide, Dr. Grant, would usually come forward and make his presence known at the beginning of a sitting through Brian's mental mediumship, often commenting on the client's health. But on this occasion Brian got up and turned the lights down, something I have never seen him do. Brian slumped in a chair and was soon in a deep trance.

The voice of Dr. Grant spoke through Brian. When I asked him about the séances in Doncaster he explained to me that all of the communicators were impersonators. This shocked me but a further explanation ensued. He explained that "like attracts like" on their side just as it does here. The medium was functioning on a very low level not known to her and as a result was drawing in a number of spirits who hovered near the earth on a very low sphere. These people were getting a kick out of pretending to be famous people, putting on accents as in the case of "Charles de Gaulle", who every time I heard his French accent I immediately thought of Colin Wilson's experience with "Raymond" who sounded for all the world like Ella Shields as "Burlington Bertie". Then, when I got down to asking about the purported communication from my father, Dr Grant explained that it *was* my father and yet at the same time it also wasn't. My father was attempting to communicate through the ectoplasmic voice box, but his communication was filtered through the fog of the phony spirit communicators who were working with Sandy. Despite the explanation, I was disappointed. I was hoping for a very good, clear and concise communication from my father. It hadn't happened. Then, following a period of silence from Brian during which time Dr Grant seemed to go away, I suddenly sat bolt upright as I heard an American accent. Brian is British and I doubt even if he tried that he could effect a good American accent.

"My name is Bill", the voice said. "Your father cannot control this medium. I am a friend of his over here and so I'm going to try to talk to you for a bit and say what he wants to say. Your father wants you to know that he loves you very much even though he had a difficult time showing it when he was on your side. He was not very affectionate and he made mistakes. We all make mistakes. But now he is going to make it up to you. You just wait and see. Things will start to happen and happen quite quickly. You've got a book coming out soon I am told. That book is going to help an awful lot of people. You have no idea the problems with have with people who come over here who believe there is no life after death. They don't realize they're dead. The religious ones are the worst. They really do believe that they have been elected for some kind of special place over here which of course is not true. It takes an awful lot of convincing to get people to turn their thinking around. We have to work with them and work with them and try and get them to see things in a much clearer light. Just because they believed in a certain way when on earth and accepted certain creeds and dogmas doesn't entitle you to a special place here. It is by your own thoughts and actions that you arrive here in a place that is best suited to you, not by what you accepted or believed while on earth. No one can "save" you.

Others may help to point the way but it is you yourself who must take the initiative and do your best, in other words do what you think is right. Trust me when I tell you that ours is not an easy job. Your father says to tell you that your book is going to help a lot of people. Of course there are going to be people who will put up obstacles but this is bound to be. You have always had an open mind your father says. You were never one to accept things blindly. Your father says you have been thinking an awful lot lately about this business of Carl Jung and why he came to see you as he surely did. I believe the medium's guide, Dr Grant, told you that like attracts like. Carl Jung was like you when he was growing up. You need to get a book and read about this. His father was a minister and when he was growing up he was told what he considered to be a lot of fairy tales. He didn't swallow any of it and neither do you. Carl Jung was very much like you and that is why he is in your band of guides. I haven't met him over here but I'm told he's on a very high sphere. Anyway, what I'm trying to say, or rather what your father is trying to say is that you are going to be like a lighthouse, a beacon. Your work is going to help point the way and help a helluva lot of people. This is something you can count on. Your work is going to go far and wide, you can count on that. Your father thinks you are going to spend a lot of time in Europe later on. Things are planned ahead so don't think they're not. Anyway I've got to go because I can't hold this medium in trance much longer."

Brian woke up and remembered nothing. Soon after the sitting with Brian Hurst I got a copy of Carl Jung's autobiography, *Memories, Dreams, Reflections*. In the chapter titled "School Years" Jung wrote:

I either did not see or gravely doubted that God filled the world with His goodness. This, apparently, was another of those points which must not be reasoned about but must be believed. In fact, if God is the highest good, why is the world,

His creation, so imperfect, so corrupt, so pitiable? This weighty tome on dogmatics was nothing but fancy drivel; worse still, it was a fraud or a specimen of uncommon stupidity whose sole aim was to obscure the truth. I was disillusioned and even indignant, and once more seized with pity for my father, who had fallen victim to this mumbo-jumbo.

I discovered on reading his book that Carl Jung was interested in Spiritualism and psychical research the same as myself from a very early age. In his chapter titled "Student Years" he writes,

The observations of the spiritualists, weird and questionable as they seemed to me, were the first accounts I had seen of objective psychic phenomena. Names like Zoellner and Crookes impressed themselves on me, and I read virtually the whole of the literature available to me at the time. Naturally I also spoke of these matters to my comrades, who to my great astonishment reacted with derision and disbelief or with anxious defensiveness. I wondered at the sureness with which they could assert that things like ghosts and table-turning were impossible and therefore fraudulent, and on the other hand at the evidently anxious nature of their defensiveness. I, too, was not certain of the absolute reliability of the reports, by why, after all, should there not be ghosts? How did we know that something was "impossible"? And, above all, what did the anxiety signify? For myself I found such possibilities extremely interesting and attractive. They added another dimension to my life; the world gained depth and background.

Like Jung, I never fit into the mould. I have been asked more than once if I believe that dogs are psychic. I definitely do. I first met my dog, Pinky in the autumn of 2011 when I was sharing a house in Rancho Mirage, California with my former radio buddy, Gene

Grant. That first day there were two dogs out back pawing at the glass to get in. "That's Pinky and Dundee," said Gene. And there was Pinky, her nose peeking out over the back wall, staring straight at me. I knew right then and there that Pinky had to be mine. I can't explain it. It's like we had known each other before and she was just waiting to come back to me. It turned out both dogs belonged to Claudia, Gene's girlfriend. And they were not allowed in the house. So as soon as everybody went to sleep, I sneaked Pinky in and she slept on my bed. She looked at me like we were together at last. It wasn't until a year later after Claudia had given me Pinky that a local psychic, Debbie Moffat, came to the house. The moment she saw Pinky she said, "You and Pinky were together in a previous life. You got split up because you died and she was left alone. Pinky is very special and you knew it from the beginning." Well when she said "you knew it from the beginning" I almost fell over. Don't forget she was someone else's dog and yet within one hour we were just inseparable.

It is a plain fact that dogs can see spirits. My deceased father would always bring the smell of cigarette smoke when he was around. Dad was a real smoker. And when he was near me Pinky would always look up and stare. I couldn't see a thing but Pinky could. I wouldn't take a million dollars for Pinky but that's a subject for another book.

As I said in the Introduction, if any of my experiences with psychic phenomena are true then we need to adopt a new world view. I do not seem to be able to share the view of my fellow human beings that the world is a fairly straightforward place. So even if I convince myself that life after death is a proven fact, I cannot accept that this has in anyway solved the riddle of human existence. If there are ghosts and if the future can be predicted before it happens, the looming question is why? Like Columbo, it always seems there will always be "just one more thing". Perhaps the information put forward in the following chapters may help us to understand more about how the Universe works.

But for now, I am going to let my "friend" Carl Jung have the last word. He writes in *Memories, Dreams, Reflections,*

> Our age has shifted all emphasis to the here and now, and thus brought daemonization of man and his world. The phenomenon of dictators and all the misery they have wrought springs from the fact that man has been robbed of transcendence by the shortsightedness of the super-intellectuals. Like them, he has fallen a victim to unconsciousness. But man's task is the exact opposite: to become conscious of the contents that press upward from the unconscious. Neither should he persist in his unconsciousness, nor remain identical with the unconscious elements of his being, thus evading his destiny, which is to create more and more consciousness. As far as we can discern, the sole purpose of human existence is to kindle a light in the darkness of mere being.

Chapter Two

Can We Explain the Poltergeist?

No living organism can continue for long to exist sanely under conditions of absolute reality. Even larks and katydids are supposed, by some, to dream. Hill House, not sane, stood by itself against its hills, holding darkness within. It had stood so for eighty years and might stand for eighty more. Within, walls continued upright, bricks met neatly, floors were firm, and doors were sensibly shut. Silence lay steadily against the wood and stone of Hill House, and whatever walked there walked alone.

Shirley Jackson
The Haunting of Hill House

In the summer of 1989, shortly after the publication of my book, *A Life Beyond Death*, I received a call from Hollywood medium Brian Hurst. He had some exciting news. He had been contacted by a family who had some unusual goings-on in their house. Writing appeared on the walls, on a bathroom mirror, objects moved by themselves and would disappear and the reappear in a different place. Brian told me he had been out to the house to determine what was going on and he came to the conclusion that they had a poltergeist. The word poltergeist is German for "noisy spirit". Brian had performed a cleansing which seemed to have had no effect. Would I be interested in meeting the family? Perhaps I could conduct an investigation of my own and maybe even get a story out of it. I immediately contacted the family who suggested that I come and stay in the house for a while with them, observe the phenomena and see what I could do to help. They would offer me accommodation and one of the family members was an excellent cook. How could I refuse?

I drove the thirty miles east of Los Angeles to what is known as the "Inland Empire" where the family resided in a large, imposing modern-style house surrounded by black wrought iron fencing and a huge gate. It was a hot August day and you couldn't keep your neck dry with a bath towel; the house itself wasn't much. It was smaller than Buckingham Palace and had fewer windows than the Chrysler Building. My thoughts flashed immediately to "Hill House", the fictitious setting of Shirley Jackson's novel about a haunted house in New England. In the novel, a college professor whose hobby is psychical research invites three people to spend the summer ghost watching in a haunted house. The professor has rented the house for the summer for the same reasons the Society for Psychical Research rented Ballechin House in Scotland in 1897 and sent Miss Ada Goodrich Freer and a few of her companions to spend the summer ghost watching and playing croquet. The investigation took on the tone of an Edwardian country house weekend, what with the rattle of teacups in the summer house, the click of croquet balls on the lawn, the swish of taffeta skirts, and spires of verbascums and delphiniums in the garden rising through mists of lavender and santolina. Once there, Miss Goodrich Freer claimed to have witnessed all kinds of unearthly phenomena, thumps, bangs, ghostly screams, phantom footsteps, and elusive presences. There was a poltergeist that tore the clothes off the bed, and a ghostly nun who was spotted by Miss Goodrich Freer in a nearby glen. Oddly enough, guests who came to stay with Miss Goodrich Freer never encountered the more terrifying phenomena, but they heard numerous bangs and footsteps. Back in London, she proceeded to write her alleged Haunting of Ballechin House but was incensed when one of her guests, a certain J. Callender Ross, beat her past the post with an with an article in the Times entitled, "On the Trail of a Ghost".

On that summer day in 1989 I stood at the gate wondering if I should go in. I wondered if I should meet the same fate as the characters in Shirley Jackson's novel, all of whom had nervous breakdowns or went mad during their ghost watching experience.

Jackson writes:

> I should have turned back at the gate, Eleanor thought. The house had caught her with an atavistic turn in the pit of the stomach, and she looked along the lines of its roofs, fruitlessly endeavouring to locate the badness, whatever dwelt there. Her hands turned nervously cold so that she fumbled, trying to take out a cigarette, and beyond everything else she was afraid.

I rang the bell at the gate and it was answered immediately by a pleasant looking, slightly overweight woman who I will call Debbie. As I made my way into their dark house, she explained that they had witnessed more phenomena that very morning. They were treated to a shower of stones falling on the roof. Showers of stones are not uncommon in poltergeist cases. There has never been an explanation for them, and upon examination the stones appear to be ordinary stones, often from a neighbour's garden.

After settling into my living quarters, which consisted of a spacious room and bath, Debbie showed me the bathroom mirror. It was a large, framed mirror hanging over the bathroom sink and on it, written in soap, were strange symbols and words. Large triangles and circles and words such as "die" and "leave" were clearly spelled out.

Debbie and her husband Bill and their three children had been enduring these paranormal pranks for three months. It didn't take long for me to discover that the goings-on in their house bore a close resemblance to one of the most famous poltergeist cases of all time, one that took place in North London in 1977. The case was investigated by Maurice Grosse and Guy Playfair of the Society for Psychical Research. In August 1977 single parent

Peggy Hodgson called the police to her home in Enfield, North London after two of her four children claimed that furniture was moving and knocking sounds were heard on walls. The children included Margaret, age 13, Janet, age 11, Johnny, age 10 and Billy, age 7. A police constable saw a chair slide on the floor by itself. Later claims included allegedly demonic voices, loud noises, thrown rocks and toys, overturned chairs and levitation of children. The focus of the paranormal events seemed to centre on the two girls, especially Janet. Young girls, especially around the age of puberty, seem to spark off poltergeist phenomena. The California family also had three young children and one of them was a girl. There were many similarities.

Society for Psychical Research members Maurice Grosse and Guy Playfair reported "curious whistling and barking noises coming from Janet's general direction". Grosse and Playfair believed that even though some of the alleged poltergeist activity was faked by the girls, other incidents were genuine. Janet was detected in trickery. A video camera caught her bending spoons and attempting to bend an iron bar. Grosse had observed Janet banging a broom handle on the ceiling and hiding his tape recorder.

As I settled in that first day and sat around their big kitchen table drinking coffee, I learned that the family had their own ideas about the cause of the phenomena. Leena was Bill's mother. She looked like she had been drinking coffee and smoking cigarettes for about sixty years. She had employed a housekeeper in a previous house she had owned and lived in. The housekeeper came from El Salvador and was believed to have practised Santeria, a form of black magic. They believed that while practising some form of ritual that she had "opened a door" to another dimension and let in some sort of demonic force. Debbie referred to it as "Mister Entity". Debbie also believed she herself possessed psychic abilities and may have been acting as a form of battery to fuel the phenomena.

It became obvious almost at once that the family was convinced that some form of "demonic possession" was responsible for the disturbances. This would play a major role later on in the investigation when "demonologists" Ed and Lorraine Warren visited the house from Connecticut at the family's expense. My meeting with Ed and Lorraine was indeed a memorable one. There is a common thread running through all of the Warren's investigations, namely that "demonic entities" were always responsible for the phenomena. The Warrens (Ed is now deceased) were Roman Catholics and their stock cure for the phenomena they investigated was an exorcism by a Catholic priest. Lorraine is a self-proclaimed medium who has never been tested for any kind of psychic abilities. The Warrens developed a reputation for investigating haunted houses. Unfortunately, they did not have an equal reputation for ridding the houses of the phenomena. The Warrens developed a rigorous belief system which was hard to shake, namely that poltergeists do not exist and that all such disturbances came from the Devil. I could not disagree more, disbelieving in the Devil.

Ralph Sarchie, in his book *Deliver Us From Evil* writes, "soon I became a regular at the Warren's Monday night classes for psychic researchers spending hours soaking up the lore of demonology."

But it was many weeks before the Warrens came to the house to conduct their investigation and at this point I was on my own. In the afternoon of my first day at the house I was sitting alone in the lounge drinking a cup of coffee when from out of nowhere a book flew out of the ceiling and hit me on the head. When I bent over to pick it up I could see that it was a copy of my recently published book, *A Life Beyond Death*. This both astonished and shocked me because the only copy of the book I had brought with me was locked in the boot of my car. My own book being hurled at me was just too much.

I was reminded of the scene in *The Haunting of Hill House*

where Dr. Montague explains to the others the kind of tricks poltergeists play including hurling books and throwing stones:

> "Poltergeists are another thing altogether," the doctor said, his eyes resting briefly on Eleanor. "They deal entirely with the physical world. They throw stones, they move objects, they smash dishes. Mrs. Foyster at Borley Rectory was a long suffering woman, but she finally lost her temper when her best teapot was hurled through the window. There is a manor in Scotland, infested with poltergeists, where as many as seventeen spontaneous fires have broken out in one day. Poltergeists like to turn people out of bed violently by tipping the bed end over end, and I remember the case of a minister who was forced to leave his home because he was tormented, day after day, by a poltergeist who hurled at his head hymn books stolen from a rival church."

Since I had assumed the role of psychic investigator I was obviously the prime target. I first suspected the children as being behind at least part of the phenomena. Perhaps they were playing tricks and it was one of the two boys or perhaps the girl who threw the book at me. In the famous Enfield poltergeist case which plagued Mrs. Harper and her two girls, investigator Guy Playfair was inclined to suspect Janet, an extremely lively little girl. He even asked Mrs. Harper to keep a special watch on her, adding, "Even if Janet is playing tricks, it may not be her fault." He had come across a curious discovery made by Dr. William Roll, namely that the focus of a poltergeist case may throw things in the ordinary way without being aware of it. Through a one-way mirror Roll saw one of his "suspects" throwing things. Yet a lie detector test showed the suspect was telling the truth when he denied throwing anything. The implication is that poltergeists can get inside someone and make them do things.

Playfair tried tying the leg of Janet's bedside chair to the leg of her bed. He used wire. Within minutes the chair had fallen over. The wire had been snapped. He bound it with several twists of wire. Not long after, the chair fell over again. The wire had been snapped. A big armchair tipped over, then the bed shot across the room. A book flew off the shelf, hit the door, proceeded at right angles, and landed upright on the floor.

The Enfield occurrences were not unlike my own in the house. Soon the phenomena took a turn and seemed to focus on me. Writing appeared on the bathroom mirror, "Gary die soon". Similar threatening writings appeared on the walls of my bedroom. I also witnessed objects moving without any apparent human intervention. As the entire family sat together in the lounge, I witnessed all the objects on a fireplace mantle instantly turn around backwards! One minute they were all facing one direction and the next minute they were all turned backwards. It was exactly like a passage in *The Haunting of Hill House*: "Nothing in this house moves," Eleanor said, "until you look away, and then you just catch something from the corner of your eye. Look at the little figurines on the shelves; when we all had our backs turned they were dancing with Theodora."

One day I was eating some Chinese food when a shadow fell over my Chop Suey. I don't know who it was or what it was but I'll never forget the feeling I had.

But what (or who) was causing these disturbances? I contacted Dr. William Roll, a parapsychologist with vast experience in poltergeist cases. Due to other commitments he was unable to come. But, unlike the family which had developed the idea that an entity induced by black magic was at work, and the Warrens, who in my opinion were blatant frauds, who preached demon possession in every case they investigated including Amityville, Roll believed that a person, usually a child, gave off some kind of energy that caused this kind of phenomena:

I do not know of any evidence for the existence of

the poltergeist as an incorporeal entity other than the disturbances themselves, and these can be explained more simply as PK effects from a flesh and blood person who is at their centre. This is not to say that we should close our minds to the possibility that some cases of RSPK might be due to incorporeal entities. But there is no reason to postulate such an entity when the incidents occur around a living person. It is easier to suppose that the central person is himself the source of the PK energy.

But how could "PK energy" account for the almost daily writings on the bathroom mirror saying that I was going to die? I was incapable of believing that the children were doing it. And since I did not believe in devil possession (and neither did world-renowned psychic Alex Tanous) that only left one explanation. A poltergeist "spirit" was causing the pranks.

Proof came in a strange way; no way were the small children responsible for the goings-on. One night I was sitting at the table eating dinner with the family when all of a sudden my hair was being cut off of my head and began falling to the floor. Everyone witnessed this. It was as though invisible scissors were being used to chop off my hair. This was too much.

At this point I began to wish that my friend, Alex Tanous, could come and investigate but he was busy teaching classes in parapsychology. It was Alex who made a complete investigation of the so-called Amityville Horror and pronounced it a complete fraud in every respect. Having learned of Alex's visit to the Amityville house, and unable to stick to the truth, Ed Warren spouted the story that Alex had levitated off the ground. This story spread faster than manure on a new lawn. So fast that Alex was forced to write to several radio stations over which the story had been broadcast.

Alex wrote:

In regards to the statement made by Ed Warren on the Brian Dow Radio Show on September 1, 1979 that I had levitated two feet off the ground in the Amityville house, which is untrue. I personally found nothing that resembled any of the paranormal things mentioned in the book. An article which appeared in the "Star" magazine after my visit said that I had said that it was demonic forces at work, which is also UNTRUE. Anyone who knows me, knows that I DO NOT BELIEVE IN DEVIL POSSESSION.

At approximately the two month mark of my staying in the house, the family contacted Ed and Lorraine Warren from Connecticut to come and try to rid the house of the manifestations. As self-proclaimed "demonologists" at every lecture they proclaimed loudly that devils and demons were at the bottom of almost every one of their investigations. In his book, *Ghost Hunters,* Ed Warren writes, "*Ghost Hunters* offers irritable proof that the demonic underworld actually exists and plays a far more prominent role in our daily lives than most of us would like to admit." I had first heard of the Warrens through psychic Alex Tanous who at that time was probably one of the most famous psychics in the world. He had been tested by the American Society for Psychical Research in New York and had a close working relationship with that organization and Dr. Karlis Osis. Alex told me he had visited the Amityville house and "thought the whole thing was a hoax". During the investigation and while interviewing the Lutzes, Alex caught a glimpse of a contract outlining the rights and gains of both the book and film promoting the alleged "haunting". This was all the investigators needed to assure themselves that their time was being wasted, and that the case should be left there and then. It was obvious from the beginning that the Warrens and myself would not like each other. Unlike Alex Tanous, Ed had no formal training in parapsychology or psychical research. Lorraine had never been formally tested as a medium and both came from a point of view that was directly opposed to mine. Alex Tanous firmly believed Amityville was a hoax. Ed Warren writes in *Ghost Hunters*, "Jay Anson's version of demonic infestation certainly squares with ours." And yet Ed made up stories and outright lied about what supposedly happened to Alex at Amityville. So much misleading information had been passed around by the Warrens about Alex that Alex wrote a letter to various radio stations to clear his name.

> Dear Sir,
> On September 1st on the Brian Dow Radio Show, called "True Inside Story of Amityville" with George Lutz, the Warrens, Rick Moran and Steve Kaplan, I understand it was stated by Steve Kaplan that Mr. Ed Warren made the statement that I had levitated two feet off the ground when I was doing the research at the Amityville house. I would like to verify if this statement was indeed made, for if it was I want you and your listeners to know that this is not true. Furthermore, in my investigation I witnessed nothing paranormal existing in the house.
> Yours truly,
> Alex Tanous

Alex was not the only one who labelled Amityville a hoax. Before I met the Warrens I did some research of my own because I wanted to know what I was getting into. Just over a year after the DeFeo murders, the house was purchased by George Lutz. Lutz had heard of the murders so he called in a priest to bless the house. The priest was supposedly driven out of the house by an angry disembodied voice, and received stigmatic blisters on his skin. The family daughter reported a pig named Jodie who later began making appearances to the rest of the family through windows. Angry red eyes looked into the house at night and left cloven footprints in the snow. George Lutz, whose business was failing, hoped to find a silver lining and called up the publisher Prentice Hall. *The Exorcist* had come out only two years before and had been wildly successful, putting things like demons and abused priests firmly in the public consciousness, so Prentice Hall was keen to capitalize on the Lutz's experience. The publisher engaged Jay Anson to write the book, *The Amityville Horror* and the rest is history. I then discovered that Lutz had a meeting with William Weber, Butch DeFeo's defence attorney. The story of the haunting was concocted, based in part upon elements from *The Exorcist*. Lutz stood to gain from the commerciality of a ghost story based upon the DeFeo murders, and Weber would have a new defence for his client. Demons, as evidenced by the Lutz's experience, caused Butch DeFeo to murder his family, at least in Butch's own mind.

Prior to the publication of the book, Lutz and Weber called a television crew from Channel 5 in New York who brought in the Warrens who reported on camera that the house was plagued with malevolent spirits. Then Steve Kaplan, the parapsychologist whom the Lutzes called in during their brief stay in the house didn't buy the Lutz's story, and concluded that he was being hoaxed. Later, when Jay Anson's book became so popular, Kaplan became concerned that the Lutz's story, which he considered bogus, would give psychical research a bad name so he wrote his own book called, *The Amityville Horror Conspiracy* in which he laid out more than one hundred factual inconsistencies.

Among these inconsistencies, Father Pecoraro, the priest who tried to bless the house when the Lutz's moved in but was allegedly attacked, reports that nothing unusual happened during his visit and no attack or evil threat of any kind took place. Some reports, including one affidavit by Pecararo himself, stated that he never visited at all but only spoke to the Lutzes over the phone. As a result, author Jay Anson created a new priest for the book, Father Mancuso. The only priest who ever got blisters and a ghostly warning was a fictitious character. No snow fell during the period, which strains the cloven hoof prints in the snow. In short the book was full of episodes that created physical evidence, but none of that alleged evidence has ever withstood any scrutiny. Everything that was falsifiable was easily falsified by Kaplan and numerous other investigators and yet the Warrens defended the Jay Anson book and lied to questioners at a lecture in which a woman stated, "I was told that the priest in the Amityville book never existed." But the questioner was told otherwise. As related in Gerald Brittle's book, *The Demonologist: The Extraordinary Career of Ed and Lorraine Warren*, Lorraine replied, "Madam, the priest in that case is a friend of ours. We know him very well. Not only did the things happen to him that were reported in the book, more things have happened to him since that were never reported." More lies from Lorraine.

The Catholic Diocese of Rockville Center and the Amityville Police Department also debunked the scam. Even the Lutzes repudiated some parts of their fantastic story. The best piece of evidence: George Weber admitted in a radio interview, and to the press, that the Amityville haunting was a hoax concocted to make money.

Let me state categorically that I do not believe in demons or the Devil. I agree with Alex Tanous that there is no such thing as devil possession. Persons with strong religious convictions like the Warrens will go to any lengths, even lie about the facts, such as Alex levitating off the ground to back up their claims.

Harry Price, who investigated the haunting at Borley Rectory, wrote in *Poltergeist Over England*, "My own view is that they are invisible, intangible, malicious and noisy entities. Poltergeists are able, by laws yet unknown to our physicists, to extract energy from living persons, often from the young, and usually from girl adolescents, especially if they suffer from some mental disorder." Most parapsychologists are of the opinion that poltergeist phenomena are examples of unconscious PK exercised by the person around whom they occur. In the case of the Enfield haunting there were young children present and in the case of the family in southern California there were three young children present. I was certain that the presence of these young children played a role in some way in aiding the phenomena. After two months of living with them and also enduring all the disturbances with them, the family and I had become friends. I told them that I knew when the Warrens arrived there would be problems between us.

The Warrens arrived on a cold winter's day without a cloud in the sky. Bright sunshine shone into all the gloomy rooms of the house and it hardly seemed like the setting for a haunting. In my opinion there are two classes of people: high class and no class. The Warrens fell into the second category. Lorraine Warren took an instant dislike to me. Lorraine was about as charming as a rattlesnake with a sore head. The family introduced me as a writer and a friend of the family who was staying with them. Lorraine almost immediately told me she thought I should leave because she thought I didn't belong there. The family came to my defence and said I was not leaving. Ed was an overweight man with a paunch that stood out like spats at an Iowa picnic.

Ed informed us that Lorraine would "walk the house" to determine what was going on. This was a reference to her presumed mediumistic powers. When Lorraine returned from "walking the house" she informed us that "there is a definite presence of evil here". Here we go again.

It was decided to conduct a séance that evening to try and make contact with entities that were causing the problems. I was particularly interested in this because I had attended genuine séances in England with real mediums and listened to recordings of independent direct voice séances with medium Leslie Flint who was able to produce the voices of deceased person in mid-space about three feet from his head while bound and gagged in various tests (more about Leslie Flint in the next chapter). In my opinion his work is the most reliable proof that we survive death

42

and go on existing in another dimension regardless of any sort of religious belief or lack of it.

The Warrens would return to their motel (paid for by the family) and come back to the house at eight o clock for the séance. The séance took place in an upstairs room, a sort of balcony affair that overlooked the lounge room down below. The six of us sat around a large wooden table. Ed, of course, was the master of ceremonies. The lights were put out and Ed announced to the spirits that they were to rap once for yes and twice for no. Was this to be like the Fox sisters in Hydesville, New York who produced rappings by cracking their toes and eventually confessed to the whole thing shortly before their deaths? Or were we to have a more genuine performance?

Ed asked various questions and spewed out orders such as "Show yourself", often adding "In the name of Jesus Christ". I could not help but wonder why not the occasional "In the name of Buddha" since they seem to have equal ranking. Well to make a long story short there were no raps at all and nothing happened. "This is just like the Amityville Horror," I said to Lorraine, "nothing happened there either."

The Warrens only had one more day left before their return to New England and the family suggested a visit to a church to speak to a priest and perhaps also go to a Mass since the Warrens were Catholic. But there were problems with this because every Catholic priest who had been contacted about the case wanted nothing to do with it. I posed a solution. I had recently been attending an Anglo-Catholic parish of the Episcopal Church, St. Mary of the Angels. I phoned the rector and set up a meeting. The priest met with us in his office and discussed the possibility of making a visit to the house for a blessing. After this a Mass was said by him in the church at a side altar. Ed attended the Mass but Lorraine refused to go in because the church was not in union with Rome despite the fact that the Mass at St. Mary's was more Catholic than the Catholic Church; she still wouldn't go in. More hypocrisy. What would the carpenter from Galilee do? Poor Jesus. St. Mary's was wearing the wrong label.

On the day of their departure Ed and Lorraine gathered in the back of the family's house and picked a huge bag of oranges to take back to New England. And that was the last I ever saw of them. It was time for me, too to depart. The strange occurrences continued on for about another year and eventually wound down and then stopped altogether. Everyone in the family is now deceased except Debbie. Before I left California for good in 2013 I had a meeting with Debbie who told me that it was all quiet now. It would seem like in Shirley Jackson's novel about Hill House that "whatever walks there walks alone".

Chapter Three

Mediumship and Life after Death

If there were to be a conscious existence after death, it would, so it seems to me, have to continue on the level of consciousness attained by humanity, which in any age has an upper though variable limit. There are many human beings who throughout their lives and at the moment of death lag behind their own potentialities and – even more important – behind the knowledge which has been brought to consciousness by other human beings during their own lifetimes.
Carl Gustave Jung
Memories, Dreams, Reflections

I was sitting in the beautiful cottage owned by the medium George Daisley in Montecito, California. George was about to give me a sitting. It was George who gave 14 mediumistic sittings to Episcopal Bishop James Pike in the 1960s. Pike, who eventually left the Episcopal Church for psychical research, was there to try and communicate with his dead son. Born in England, George Daisley came to California in 1960. As soon as I settled into a comfortable chair George went into a sort of trance and began scribbling on a piece of paper. When he handed it to me it was unreadable. "The writing is backwards," he said. "Hold it up to the mirror." When I held it up to a mirror it was clearly legible. It said, "We give you love from Betty and Stewart Edward White." This was amazing. I had read some of Mr. White's books and even had one on my bedside table. From about 1900 until about 1922 he wrote fiction and non-fiction about adventure and travel, with an emphasis on natural history and outdoor living. Starting in 1922 he and his wife Elizabeth "Betty" Grant White wrote numerous books they say were received through séances with spirits. They also wrote of their travels around the state of California.

After the sitting George told me all about his meetings with Bishop Pike. Pike had resigned as Episcopal Bishop of California and had come to see Daisley in the hope of communicating with his son who had committed suicide. "I gave Pike 14 sittings," George told me, "and provided enough evidence for the bishop to where he came to accept that he was in communication with his son."

Throughout the 1960s Pike continued his exploration into the unknown. He held a séance in Canada with medium Arthur Ford which made front-page news. Always a renegade, Pike eventually left the Episcopal Church. In an interview with talk show host Joe Pyne when asked:

"Don't you believe that Christ ascended into heaven and sat at the side of his Father?" Pike stated in reply, "Ascended where? Heaven. Where's that? Since Copernicus? Before Copernicus it was heaven above, hell below, stars, moon and sun hanging like Christmas tree decorations, and a geocentric parochialism. No, I don't believe that he sat there at all. I don't believe in these physical images. Earth was thought to be the centre of everything before Copernicus. Now we can't look at things that way, and we can't any more, since Copernicus, talk about up and down and all those things. No I don't believe in the ascension of Jesus in heaven. I believe that he continued in personal ongoing life like all of us will and that this was known by those who were closest to him, and that these experiences they had of him were genuine experiences of him."

Pyne then asked, "Where will eternity find you?" and Pike answered,

"Good question. When I die I will be the same Jim Pike I am now, living on and on with the hangups that I have and barriers and blocks that continue to be worked on through encounters. Every encounter is a chance to grow or shrivel. So when I die I will be just the Jim Pike I am now, who has grown some, various breakthroughs have occurred. I, too, have shown that I can be a servant sometimes. I have gotten rid of some idols out of my life. Those that still remain I still have to get rid of, in freedom. God doesn't arm twist."

Jim Pike was way ahead of his time. The Church wasn't ready for him. He died in the desert when I was in high school in 1969. Just like Carl Jung, Pike is one of my heroes. He was down to earth. He didn't sugar coat things. He said what he felt and he felt it deeply. He wanted to change things. When there was no room for change.

I feel he wanted to be remembered for the good that he did and the people that he helped rather than as a "heretic". In his goodbye address in Grace Cathedral in San Francisco he said, "If there was no Virgin Birth and no ascension into heaven, what CAN a man believe?"

Which brings me to the point of this chapter. The debate about whether we live after we die has been going on for centuries. I believe I can answer the question, "Will it ever come out and be scientifically proven that there is a life after death, and will that proof reveal what really happens?" The answer is probably no. Why? For the same reason that we will probably never have free energy and will continue to depend on fossil fuels. There is too much at stake to tell the truth. First of all, the Church would collapse. It has existed for centuries on promoting fear and guilt and a dependence on fantastic belief systems. To quote Mike Fearon in a Leslie Flint direct voice séance in the mid 1960s:

The things people actually believe are quite fantastic. In fact, far more fantastic than the actual truth about the world we live in after death. People don't suddenly become angels or meet Jesus when they die. And yet the Church continues to crank out this same pabulum year after year, heaven if you have been awfully good and practised what they believe to be true, and hell if you haven't. The fact of the matter is that it doesn't hold water at all.

I am reminded of another Flint session where a Salvation Army lady came through and researcher Betty Greene, knowing their beliefs asked her, "Well, have you met Jesus?" and the reply was, "No, I have not met him yet but I am sure I will, he must be here someplace."

The truth would upset everything. As crop circle researcher Michael Glickman says, "Would you want to have to be the one to announce to the world, "It's proven. Earth is round!?" Of course you wouldn't because it would disturb everybody." "Everybody wants everything to be the way it was yesterday," Glickman says and he is right. This is the reason why only a handful of scientists since the nineteenth century have ventured into the area of psychical research, for fear of ridicule and damage to their careers. People like Sir William Crookes and Sir Oliver Lodge went out on a limb but few today will do that. It is easier to be a debunker. Even in the face of mountains of evidence for the near death experience, in which many actually saw themselves on a surgical table and listened to conversations between doctors while they were clinically dead and were able to report those conversations later, there are still people like Susan Blackmore who cannot bear to admit that there is a possibility of life after death. Blackmore dismisses the NDE as oxygen deprivation to the brain.

Shirley MacLaine tells how moved she was when, sitting in the back of a mock-up limousine on the set of *Being There*, her fellow actor Peter Sellers told her about his near death experience. He had had a heart attack while on the set, and had floated outside his body and was taken to hospital. He was not concerned, since it was only his body that was involved. He watched a surgeon cut out his heart and massage it. Then he saw a white light above him, and felt "there was love, real love, on the other side of the light". A hand reached through the light, and at the same time he heard the surgeon say that his heart was beating again. Then a voice from the light said, "Go back and finish. It's not time." Then he found himself back in his body.

James Randi, a professional debunker, who makes a living by tearing down anything remotely paranormal, is another one who would not admit to facts even if proven scientifically.

Other professional debunkers are Joe Nickell and Michael Shermer. Shermer stated publically in an interview, "What science knows is that nothing happens after you die." Really? I guess he skipped over the work of Dr. Kenneth Ring at the University of Connecticut. Following the publication of Raymond Moody's book, *Life After Life*, Ring set out to track down and interview scores of people who had come close to death, and studied the results statistically. In all important respects, Rings findings confirmed Moody's. So did those of other researchers: Michael Sabom, Edith Fiore, Maurice Rawlings, Margot Grey.

Ring writes,

I do believe – but not just on the basis of my own or other's data regarding near-death experiences – that we continue to have a conscious existence after our physical death and that the core experience does represent its beginning, a glimpse of things to come.

Shermer continues, "You don't go anywhere. You're gone. We know this for a fact!" Really? Who is "we"? And what research have you done in your life on this subject? Perhaps you also skipped over the 850 out of body experiments in New York with Alex Tanous and Dr. Karlis Osis as well. A series of very carefully designed experiments were set up in which Alex One would leave his body and go to a special device and view the symbol determined by a random number generator. Proving that Alex Two could exist apart from his physical body. Shermer blathers on, "You never come back. We know that your memories and your personality are stored in your neurons in your brain. No brain, no mind, no soul."

Back to the argument that the mind and the brain are the same thing. George Meek, a North Carolina researcher who was an early pioneer in two-way electronic voice communication with the dead, and who I will discuss at greater length in a later chapter, writes,

One of the greatest blocks modern man has in understanding life after death stems from being told that brain and mind are synonymous. However, a different picture emerges for those serious researchers into the nature of man who can look beyond conventional notions. For such scientists it has become increasingly obvious that the brain and mind are *not* the same. Interpenetrating our physical body there is another body, made up of a large number of energy fields.

Each of these collects and organizes cells into shapes or organs precisely the same way a magnet organizes the thousands of iron filings into a specific pattern. For centuries occult literature has called this vast collection of energy fields the etheric body. Life after death has been studied by scientists at Southampton University who found evidence that conscious awareness can continue after death. The medical study is the largest ever into near-death and out-of-body experiences. In the largest such study ever conducted, researchers have found evidence that consciousness continues even after brain activity has ceased.

This evidence of life after death came from a study led by researchers from the University of Southampton and published in the journal *Resuscitation*.

Shermer continues, "Religions have sold people on the idea that when your loved one dies, he or she goes on." My question is why does life after death have to have anything at all to do with religion? We've come a long way since 1950.

UFO researcher Stanton Friedman says, "You really shouldn't expound your ideas on any of these subjects unless you have done some research of your own. Every day I come across people who are self-appointed experts and yet they have done no research at all."

Another debunker who has conducted no research is Joe Nickell. He says, "I think we have to look at the hard facts. You need your brain, I need my brain, when we think, walk, do anything. The idea that we don't really need our brain, that it's just sort of an incidental thing, we might use it or we might not, is ludicrous."

I agree that we have to look at the hard facts. So why isn't he looking at them instead of spouting this nonsense? "So when you die, and I'm not talking about marginal cases where somebody might be revived, I'm talking about really dead, decomposed, that's the destruction of the brain and there's going to be no brain activity."

Independent EEG studies have confirmed that the brain's electrical activity, and hence brain function, ceases at that time. But seven out of 63 (11 per cent) of the Southampton patients who survived their cardiac arrest recalled emotions and visions during unconsciousness.

Interestingly, the old challenge from sceptical scientists that after-death experiences were simply the result of near-death hallucinations caused by medication or oxygen-starvation are now just about completely refuted. The quoted report of the University of Southampton research briefly also raises this same point:

There are currently three explanations for these accounts. The first is physiological; that the hallucinations patients experience is due to disturbed brain chemistry caused by drug treatment, a lack of oxygen or changes in carbon dioxide levels.

In the Southampton study none of the four patients who had near-death experiences had low levels of oxygen or received any unusual combination of drugs during their resuscitation.

It might also be added that 'technically after death' consciousness experiences right across many countries and cultures show a remarkable similarity.

Dr Kenneth Ring Ph.D, who is Professor Emeritus of Psychology at the University of Connecticut, and Sharon Cooper completed a two-year study into the NDEs of the blind. They published their findings in a 1999 book entitled *Mindsight* in which they documented the solid evidence of 31 cases in which blind people report visually accurate information obtained during an NDE. Perhaps the best example in his study is that of a forty-five year old blind woman by the name of Vicki Umipeg. Vicki was born blind, her optic nerve having been completely destroyed at birth because of an excess of oxygen she received in the incubator. Yet, she appears to have been able to see during her NDE. Her story is a particularly clear instance of how NDEs of the congenitally blind can unfold in precisely the same way as do those of sighted persons.

Oops, Joe. I guess you never read this material. Why is change so threatening? Because as Michael Glickman has said, "Everybody wants everything to be the way it was yesterday."

The truth is that many of the psychology researchers who are involved in these studies into near-death and after-death consciousness claims have a strong Christian background but they have been finding that when they want to discuss their increasingly amazing findings with Christian ministers and writers they are having the door slammed in their faces! Is that not incredible? Many times some of the results of this research is only being carefully documented on psychic-type, New Age and even occult-type websites because Christians will still not discuss or openly acknowledge some of these things! Of course, the fact that much of the available research data is now posted on psychic-type websites just continues to perpetuate the belief of many Christians, especially evangelical Christians, that this whole area is somehow associated with the activity of demons! Moreover, once perfectly honest claims get in the hands of supporters of things like the occult and reincarnation there is always a serious danger of such claims being "embroidered" – and I have no doubt that this has occasionally happened.

What we can say is that it is surely time that evangelical Christianity opened its eyes on this subject and started to consider the real possibility that a phenomenon which is so world-wide and which so many people have experienced (yes, and which so many have strongly associated with heaven and with Jesus, even if they had not previously been religious-types – they do not usually associate the experience with demons!), may have real validity?

Some of the most interesting information on verifiable after-death consciousness experiences has been gathered by Dr Melvin Morse who is Associate Professor of Pediatrics at The University of Washington. Dr Morse has studied near-death experiences in children for 15 years and is the author of several books on the subject. In 1982, while a Fellow for the National Cancer Institute, Dr. Morse was working in a clinic in Pocatello, Idaho. He was called to revive a young girl who nearly died in a community swimming pool. She had had no heart beat for 19 minutes, yet completely recovered. She was able to recount many details of her own resuscitation, and then said that she was taken down a brick-lined tunnel to a heavenly place. When Dr. Morse showed his obvious scepticism, she patted him shyly on the hand and said: "Don't worry, Dr. Morse, heaven is fun!"

I guess Joe missed that one too. There is no experience like a first-hand experience and I have had many of them. I have had sittings with many mediums, some good some not so good. I have to concede that some mediums are blatant frauds but that does not water down the evidence for the good ones. I am reminded of Stanton Friedman's comment, "Some UFOs are alien spacecraft. Most are not, but I don't care about those. Not all isotopes are fissionable, I don't care about those either." Thanks Stan.

The problem is that psychic work is largely measured in the public consciousness by one or two bad examples of "mediumship". You cannot say that all mediumship is hocus pocus just because you had a bad experience watching a TV medium like James Van Praagh, who has been caught cheating over and over again, or his fellow TV "medium" John Edward. This is not mediumship. I can also throw out twenty names until I get a hit and give you a great cold reading but this is not mediumship. At least not the kind of mediumship which I have been exposed to.

Tony Stockwell and Gordon Smith (formally known as the "psychic barber") are mental mediums working in England today. As far as I know, they are the only reliable mental mediums working today. Both have long waiting lists. There are no genuine physical mediums living anymore. Leslie Flint was the last one. He died in 1994. He had the rare gift of the independent direct voice, a type of mediumship where the voice of the communicator is heard in space and does not come from the mouth of the medium. There are around fifty recordings on YouTube of his séances which were given in the 1960s and 1970s with two independent researchers, George Woods and Betty Greene. They sat with Flint every Monday morning for 15 years and collected the largest body of evidence for life after death in the world. Communicators told what happened when they died and just where they found themselves after they died. Flint was tested by the Society for Psychical Research and made to hold coloured water in his mouth and spit it out at the end of the sitting; he was also bound and gagged. This did not prevent the voices from speaking.

David Thompson, a supposed "physical medium" who lives in Australia is supposed to be able to produce materializations. Genuine materialization séances, including the one I attended in 1966, take place in strong red light. Thompson refuses all offers to be tested and his séances take place in total darkness. You make up your own mind.

Nothing beats a surprise, especially if it is a pleasant one. I got the surprise of my life in 1990 while visiting London. One of the best known and most reliable mediums of the time was Albert Best. This man was phenomenal. I had been visiting a Spiritualist Church during my stay in London, the London Spiritual Mission. At times Albert Best would give demonstrations of his mediumship there. One morning I received a call at my hotel from the church. Albert Best was just on his way back from India and was stopping there for a few hours. Could I jump in a taxi and come right away, he would give me a sitting. I could and I did.

When I arrived at the church I was greeted by Mr. Best who began the sitting right away with no preliminary chatter. "Well your father is here," he began "and he wants you to know that he loves you very much. He was not able to show it in life but where he is now he is able to see his past mistakes." My father was a good father but he did not show much emotion. I never got many hugs and kisses. "Tell my son I love him, please tell my son," he said. The sitting went on to describe all sorts of verifiable things such as the fact that I had been living in a small cottage in Vermont, that my mother had remarried and that there were problems between us. At the end of one hour I got up, I had gone through four or five tissues. "How much do I owe you?" I asked. "Five pounds, give it to the church." Albert Best WAS the best and he was not a medium who charged fancy prices for his sittings. Sadly, he is with us no more.

On a warm summer day in the 1980s I found myself sitting on a bus from Boston to Portland, Maine. As I got off the bus I was greeted by Alex Tanous with whom I had developed a deep friendship while writing my book *A Life Beyond Death*. We became good friends and remained so until his death from cancer in July 1990. At the time I was living in Vermont and often would go up to Maine and spend a week with Alex. As I got off the bus I received a warm hug from Alex. Alex loved to hug people. We would always go to the IHOP, the International House of Pancakes for breakfast. On this occasion I had come to interview Alex about his experiences that formed his conclusions about life after death. They were many. Alex was born with the ability to split himself in two, into Alex One and Alex Two. He had the first experience of this in childhood:

My first experience was the most traumatic. It happened at the age of five. My mother was carrying a kettle of boiling water. She accidentally tripped and the boiling water splashed all over me. I was not burned by the water. My parents decided to take me to the family doctor, who examined me and found nothing wrong with me. He suggested that I get some rest and see how I would be the next day.

As I started climbing the stairs, I looked up. I saw myself at the top of the stairs, not clearly, but I knew it was me. I waved and the other self waved back to me. Our friendship grew, and lasted several years. As time went on, the other self became clearer and I saw it was my double. I adopted him as my imaginary playmate.

It was this experience which led me, in later years to many out of body experiences, unlike those of others, in which I had seen myself and my double, all at the same time. It was a strange experience. This also had an everlasting effect on me. I was caught, in some way, in a triangle. I have never heard of anyone else having this kind of experience.

I was so impressed by Alex's account of what happened to him that I went looking for other cases. I found them. It is important to note that there is a difference between this kind of experience that takes place when people are alive and fully awake and the NDE or Near Death Experience.

It would seem from many cases which I have studied that the body which we find ourselves in when we die is with us all along. Some people, like Alex, seem to be able to have the experience of separating from the physical while still alive. In fact, there is evidence of spontaneous and induced occurrences of astral projection as far back as the turn of the nineteenth century. When Sylvan Muldoon published his *Case for Astral Projection* in 1925, Dr A. O. Ostby had been having spontaneous cases of astral projection a quarter of a century before. Ostby, a Protestant minister, writes in his account:

I awoke one night in full clear consciousness. I found myself standing in front of the bed looking up at my own physical body. I thought I had died, but was perfectly happy and had a strong desire in this new state of freedom. But just then I thought it would be dreadful for my wife to awaken and find my lifeless form beside her. So I determined that I must try to reanimate my lifeless form. At that moment the spiritual "myself" was lifted right off the floor, laid horizontally and pushed slowly into the physical again. After that experience I acquired the ability to go in and out at will. I could lie on my couch and my double would go out without my being conscious of the separation. I would think it was my physical self until I would discover the physical body still on the couch. Then I would go to the window, see the traffic in the street, and finally enter my body again.

And there are other accounts. In *The Mystery of the Human Double*, H. P. Okeden writes,

> Whenever I desire to know where a friend is, I go and find him. It is done when awake, either sitting quietly in my chair or before going to sleep at night. Perfect quiet is necessary. I close my eyes, and have a feeling of going over backwards, and I find myself going down a long, dim tunnel. At the far end is a tiny speck of light which grows as I approach into a larger square and I am there. I can describe the room my friends are in, the clothes they are wearing, the people to whom they are talking, etc. On several occasions when I have been anxious about a friend who lives in London, I have found myself in a strange room among strange people in the country, and there was my friend. Only once have I been seen and addressed. I have been tested over and over again when I have arranged to go. One friend put on a new evening gown, another moved her bedroom furniture around, which I at once noticed and questioned her about later.

Alex Tanous was one of those people who loved to find the answers even if he wasn't sure there were any. He participated in countless experiments which were designed to show that some part of us separates from the physical, and survives death. Some of these experiments were designed by Dr. Karlis Osis in New York at the American Society for Psychical Research.

Alex told me how:

> At the age of eleven, I had another traumatic experience. This one closely copied the traditional Near Death Experience. I was rushed to the hospital for surgery. Suddenly I found

myself out of body. I saw my physical body on the table. I saw my double standing nearby, and both of us watched the doctors and nurses operating on me.

Then all at once everything disappeared. I encountered a dark line which I went through. I found myself in a beautiful light. This light came toward me and began to fill me, and then all was clear before me. I saw people I knew and some I did not know. I looked at myself, and the light had created something upon me, like a robe. I was living a beautiful experience. I remember nothing else. When I awoke, it was to the music of the Armistice Day Parade.

Through the years, I have had countless experiences taking place, but the challenge came when I was asked by Dr. Osis if I could do it at will.

James Kidd was an Arizona prospector who left a sizeable amount of money for some kind of proof of the soul. James Kidd was supposed to be a nobody, relegated to the heaps of history as just another anonymous soul, a lost copper miner. Born on July 18, 1879, in Ogdensburg, New York, Kidd disappeared in the spectacular Superstition Mountains of Arizona in November of 1949. Just another lost employee of the Miami Copper Company of Arizona. There was even some speculation among the locals that Kidd was onto a gold find and someone may have killed him to stake the claim. Kidd, a loner with no known friends or relatives, had some very valuable stock certificates in a company known as E. F. Hutton.

But nobody knew that when he never returned from his prospecting hike.

That could or should have been the end of it. Legal paperwork sprung up after his death, at the time, totally routine. In 1954, State record showed that he was a missing person.

Everything changed in 1957. Money will do that. His unclaimed safety deposit box was opened by the tax authorities.

For reasons only a bureaucrat could explain, it wasn't until 1964 that an inventory was taken. A 1930 hand-written will was found, signed in Douglas, Arizona. After inventory of the stock, the estate flowing from the safety deposit box was valued at just over $500-thousand (estate-chaser attorneys were at the front of the line: by the time the court cases were over, only $200-thousand was left).

If Alex Tanous was one of a kind so was Kidd. His will read:

This is my first and only Will and is dated the second of January, 1946. I have no heirs and have not been married in my life and after all my funeral expenses have been paid and one hundred dollars to some preacher of the gospel to say farewell at my grave, sell all my property which is all in cash and stocks with E. F. Hutton Co., Phoenix, some in safety deposit box, and have this balance money to go in a research or some scientific proof of a soul of the human body which leaves at death I think in time there can be a photograph of soul leaving the human at death. "James Kidd."

That kind of money was enough to draw the mice from the walls.

First up was the University of Life Church Inc. of Arizona who asserted: "We can do that."

Two men from Canada stepped forward claiming to be long-lost brothers of the $500K-er, James Kidd.

From May to October, 1965, Justice Robert Myers of the Court of Maricopa County, Arizona presided over ninety days of hearing including every charlatan half a million dollars could muster. Some newspapers called it the Ghost Trial of the Century.

Finally, in October 20, 1967, the money was given to the Barrow Neurological Institute, Phoenix, Arizona.

But after an additional six years of litigation it went to the American Society for Psychical Research. "The Kidd legacy was not only a windfall," wrote Nicholas Wade in Science, "but proved the parapsychologists could at least convince a court of the seriousness of their intentions."

Once the ASPR started working with the Kidd money, things started heating up with Alex as the psychic in the hot seat:

- Two experiments were designed for me to do. The first was the Optical Image Device. This is a structure about 2x2x3 feet, inside which is a rotating disc divided into four quadrants, a small picture will appear. Each time the switch is thrown, one out of five possible target images is randomly selected and becomes visible on the disc. The quadrant and its colour are also randomly selected. The equipment is designed so that no one, including the experimenters, knows the final combination of quadrant, colour, and image during the experiment. The only way to see the whole thing is by looking through the small window in front of the Optical Image device. After the session, the experimenter decodes the information from the automatic recording machine to find out what the targets were.

- This experiment took lots of hard work, but one day, I found the criteria. I experienced myself, out of body, as a spot of consciousness. I felt like a light. First this light is large, and then it comes to a point like a needle. I had the sensation of an "I am" feeling. My scoring patterns were consistent with the OBE hypothesis: that there is something that can leave the body, some consciousness which could be thought of as leaving the body at death. My score was significant.

Alex told me that he no longer looked upon himself as just Alex, but rather as Alex and Alex Two. I was impressed that he was working with a prestigious organization like the ASPR. Twenty-five years after Alex's death, the results of these significant and important tests have not been released to or studied by mainstream science for the very reasons I spoke of at the beginning of this chapter. Everybody wants everything to be the way it was yesterday.

"The results of the tests," Alex told me:

- ...led them to the second experiment with the colour wheel. This device is based upon a different optical principle, to help distinguish between different modes of perception. It is a sort of enclosed roulette wheel about 14 inches in diameter. In this case, the target is a coloured image on a black background. The only way to see the target correctly is to look precisely through the small window on the top of the box. Once again, I achieved a significant score in the experiment.

Alex Two has been seen by more than one person while Alex One was in a completely different place. Perhaps the most amazing account of this kind of bi-location took place in Canada. Alex remembered it because it frightened several people and a dog:

I was in New York at the ASPR. It was about two o'clock in the morning. I had just returned back from a date, and I was lying on the bed. Suddenly I find myself in Canada at my friend Ellsworth DeMerchant's house in a raging snowstorm. Now, I'm aware of this but I'm not aware that he's aware of me at this point. I knocked on the glass in his door, and his dog starts to bark. His wife called out to him that someone was at the door. At this point Ellsworth comes out, sees me and opens the door. We had a conversation and he invited me in. Now at this point the dog tried to bite me, so he went to put the dog in, and when he came back I was gone. So Ellsworth is wondering what has happened ... where I've gone ... and he's waiting. He is determined at this point to go out and see what happened to me. He opens the door, goes out, and there are no footprints in the snow … no car, nothing. Remember now that there is a blinding snowstorm going on.

The next morning he told his wife the story and she didn't believe him. But it was all spontaneous.

I should add at this point that Ellsworth DeMerchant was an official high up in the Canadian government. He was not the sort of person to make up strange tales.

This chapter would not be worth writing unless I were to discuss the work of independent direct voice medium Leslie Flint who died in 1994. I first encountered Flint during the writing of my book, *A Life Beyond Death.* I wrote to him that I was using portions of texts of various direct voices séances that he had given in the 1960s and 1970s and sent him a cheque for one hundred pounds as compensation. Flint would never have come, as he did, into the public eye if it were not for the work of two independent researchers, George Woods and Betty Greene. Woods was a World War I veteran who had seen hundreds of men die on the battlefield. Woods joined the Society for Psychical Research in London. There he met Charles Drayton Thomas, who had turned his investigations in a new direction: direct voice phenomena. Thomas introduced Woods to Britain's leading direct voice medium, Leslie Flint.

Woods learned that Flint was said to possess a strange and very rare gift, the ability to produce the life voice of the discarnate person through an artificially created voice box. This voice box, he was told, was produced from a substance called ectoplasm, which was drawn from the medium and his sitters while sitting in total darkness.

Woods went for a sitting. Several voices spoke to him, including his father's. From the information they gave him and the sound of the voices themselves, Woods decided they were genuine. He was told that quite soon he would meet a woman who would help him with his research.

As the years passed, Woods forgot the prediction. Then, in June 1953, a full seven years later, a woman called about a flat he had advertised in his home in Barclay Road, Croydon. The woman's name was Betty Greene.

Betty Greene turned out to be a divorcee who shared many of Wood's interests. When she moved into Wood's flat, she had no idea that one day she would be holding conversations with famous people who had died decades ago.

In 1955, by which time George Woods and Betty Greene had been sitting with Flint at regular intervals for the better part of two years, a female voice came through: that of Ellen Terry, a queen of the stage in Edwardian England, who had died in 1928.

The voice which claimed to be Ellen Terry's indicated that their work was only about to begin:

> You are going to have some remarkable communications and I suggest you keep this contact regularly to build up the power and strengthen the link which has deliberately been arranged for your tapes. There are souls on this side of life with a great desire to make use of these opportunities to pass through information about life in our world and the mechanics of communication between your world and ours.

It is a shame that this mediumship and these recordings are not more widely known. Nigel Woods, the son of George Woods sent me about fifty of his father's original reel-to-reel recordings of the direct voice séances in 1995 when I was living in Los Angeles. I played them to my discussion group in Hollywood. Most were amazed that they had never heard of Leslie Flint. On a trip to England in 1998, I went to the house in Worthing, East Sussex where George Woods and Betty Greene once lived. I stood in the road and said to myself, "this is where it all began."

I will discuss these recordings in more detail in a later chapter but for now, this is what Ellen Terry said to George and Betty on a cold December Day in 1963:

Here that which man has created will change according to him, according to his striving and his uplifting himself from the darkness. Man dwells oft-times in darkness of his own creating. As soon as he begins to desire a spark of life eternal, so he will be helped and guided and given instruction and shown the path.

No one need fear, for this is a world of love and true brotherhood. This is a world of love in which all who dwell are seeking to uplift themselves from stage to stage in the evolution.

This is a world created by the thought and beauty of expression of life that is so far removed from the material ideas and ideals. Be patient. But above all strive to overcome the worser self, endeavouring to see. Cast aside all that which holds you back, for to have fear is a bad thing indeed.

Death is the Great Door through which we all find the world of reality. There is no death, only that which seems so. Man himself has created death in ignorance and in foolishness. One day he will find, as I and others have found, the way of freedom, the way of truth, the way of life, the path that leads to God.

Chapter Four

The Problem of Religion

Something else that can be jettisoned is the accumulated, non-productive religious dogma that has ruined countless lives over the centuries, to the extent that it imposed burdens of fear and guilt.
George Meek

I was sitting in the rectory of Blessed Sacrament Roman Catholic Church in Jamaica Plain, Massachusetts. Father Richard Messina was sitting across from me. I had met Father Messina through astrologer Isabel Hickey in Watertown, Massachusetts with whom I had spent several years in the study of the science of astrology. More about Isobel in a later chapter. I was going through a very difficult time. I had just broken up with a girlfriend. To me, it seemed we had a very romantic relationship including intimacy. She had asked me if I had a lot of girlfriends before. I told her sure I have been pretty busy: At the monastery praying with the other monks. I guess she didn't get the joke. Then at some point a lot of strange things began happening. I would be sitting in her apartment and the phone would ring. She would answer it and then hang up saying there was nobody there. This happened repeatedly. Then one day I found out who was doing the calling. It was the man she was engaged to be married to; some bozo of a guy, who was a bouncer at a local bar. I don't know whether I was in love with her or I just wanted to help her out. Ever since I saw that movie *King Kong* I've been a sucker for a girl who fell for a gorilla. This was just too much. I was very broken up and in a desperate emotional state. Isobel, who we called "Issie", told me "You must go see Father Messina". Naturally I wondered why an astrologer would be sending me to a Catholic priest. Issie told me that Father Messina was also a psychic and did readings in the rectory. He kept this a closely guarded secret from the Church authorities inasmuch as if it were to be discovered that he was doing this sort of thing he would probably be kicked out of the priesthood. Inasmuch as I was not able to comprehend how a Catholic priest could give psychic readings, Issie made the appointment for me. As I sat in the rectory in front of Father Messina on that summer day I hardly knew what to expect. He certainly looked like an ordinary priest and not a psychic. As I settled into a comfortable chair, Father Messina began to tell me that he had the ability to read past lives by going into a sort of trance. At this I nearly fell off the chair. Past lives and reincarnation were directly opposed to Church teaching. How could this priest be leading a dual life, on one hand working as a parish priest and on the other hand giving past-life readings? We decided to leave that discussion for later and Father Messina began the reading. He sat behind the desk and his head sort of slumped down. He began talking in a slow, melodious voice. He told me that in a past life my girlfriend and I had been together. Only in that life she was a man and I was a woman. He said this lifetime was sometime around CE 1200. In that life the roles were reversed, she (who was a he) was in love with me but I just used her for sex, and in this lifetime I was in love with her and she used me for sex. He told me that human beings have lived hundreds of lives both as men and women in order to gain a different experience in each lifetime. We had endured an experience in that past lifetime, and now, in this lifetime, we had met gain to balance the karma. It sounded like what goes around comes around. He stressed that I should realize that now the books were balanced and that I should put it behind me and move on with my life, not linger on the experience. "The karma with her is over," he said. "Move on." As he came out of trance, I admitted that I had many questions. I asked him how he, as a Catholic priest, could lead a double life. "How can you honestly, knowing what you know, continue to crank out Church teaching and deliberately mislead people?" I felt that with the gift that Father Messina had, that this was a cheat and said so. Father Messina said that if people knew that they would have the opportunity to come back and live again in another life that the Church felt that people would lead sinful lies, knowing that they would not be in hell, but on a path of eternal progression. He told me that reincarnation had deliberately been removed from the Bible and that any and all passages that referenced reincarnation were either modified or discarded. In fact, he pointed out the passage in the New Testament in which the disciples of Jesus meet a man who was born blind. The disciples ask, "Who has sinned, this man or his parents that he was born blind?" If the man was born blind how could he have sinned unless it was in a previous lifetime?

I strongly disagreed with Father Messina. For centuries the Church had been lying to people about reincarnation and here was a Catholic priest who could condone it all. In essence he was saying it was fine to tell people privately about these things but he must go along publicly with Church doctrine. When I phoned him years later after *A Life Beyond Death* was published he refused to discuss the subject. It was like trying to open a sardine can after you've broken off the metal lip. Father Messina now has his own parish and is pastor of a church in the Archdiocese of Boston, St Mary's. Look him up.

In the hundreds of direct voice recordings that I have listened to, there seems to be a common thread running through them all, namely that all of life is an eternal progression. The Archbishop of Canterbury, Cosmo Lang returned in a Leslie Flint sitting to say:

Your world is the training ground. You have been given bodies to inhabit that through them you might experience many things. You have been given opportunity to overcome, and many fail. Indeed all fail, for no man can hope to achieve all things in the brief span on earth.

During his time on earth, Lang decided to investigate mediumship and appointed a committee under the Bishop of Bath and Wells to study the matter and report their findings. But when he discovered that the findings were favourable, he decided to forgo publishing the report, and it was thrown into a filing cabinet, where it was eventually discovered and published in 1969 as *The Findings of Archbishop Lang's Committee on Spiritualism*.

The attitude of Lang and the other bishops who wrote the report is reflective of that of many scientists and clergy today. They are afraid if the truth gets out they will be ruined. One modern day churchman who seemed to agree with me was the late Right Reverend Mervyn Stockwood, who was the Bishop of Southwark. In his introduction to Ena Twigg's book, *Ena Twigg: Medium*, he writes:

> I believe that the reason for its nonpublication was the timidity of Archbishop Lang and his colleagues. They preferred to conceal the report rather than face its implications. This timidity is characteristic not only of churchmen but of many others. They fear that if they show sympathy, they may be regarded as quacks. I remember a distinguished physiologist at Cambridge telling me that he would have nothing to do with psychical research; he refused to read its books, be present at its meetings, or take part in its tests, as the whole subject was taboo and not intended for serious minds. I suppose he would have said much the same about landing on the moon had he lived a hundred years ago.

Just like Father Messina, who is afraid to come out of the closet at a time when coming out of the closet is most needed. The Churches are in dire straits. Church attendance is at an all-time low. Whoever said that it is difficult to teach an old dog new tricks was certainly right. Nowhere was this more in evidence than in a direct voice session in which Betty Greene interrogated Father O'Leary, a nineteenth-century Irish priest who fell down a well and broke his neck. Here for the first time is a complete transcript of that conversation from a Leslie Flint direct voice sitting August 1964:

Betty Green: Hello.

Father O Leary: Hello. Hello. Can you hear?

BG: I can hear you very well, thank you.

FOL: Good. You must forgive me if I don't manage to speak very well. This is quite an experience. I'm very interested indeed in the work that you're doing. It's a puzzling business but I thought if it was possible I would come and speak to you for a moment. My name is O'Leary. I know it does not ring a bell and there's no reason why it should. I'm Father O' Leary, at least I should say I was Father O'Leary many years ago. Of course, I've been here many years now. I've changed, I've changed, as indeed do we all change. This is a very interesting thing. If it had occurred during my lifetime I would not have believed it was possible. But here I am speaking to you from the so-called dead.

BG: Father O'Leary, can you tell me how you passed over and your reactions?

FOL: Well, it has a touch of humour about it. And I expect if I tell you, you'll hardly believe it. But it's true. I suppose it is a funny thing when you come to think about it, but it's perfectly true. I fell down a well many years ago and I broke my neck. It was an old well, a disused well that had been covered up, and I was out in the night. I had been to see a sick person and on my way back I took what I thought was a short cut which I'd taken many times before. And it was dark and it was a dreadful night. I walked into this well which had not been properly attended to and I fell down the well and I broke my neck. It was tragic, but now it does not matter. And they searched for me for weeks and

70

weeks and they couldn't understand about the disappearance of the Father. It took them months before they discovered me. Oh, it was a long time ago.

BG: What were you doing in the meantime? Were you helping to search and trying to help them find you?

FOL: Yes, I tried. I was, I suppose you'd call it, earth-bound. No one seemed to notice me, and then one woman who was very psychic, at least I realize now she was very psychic, we used to think she was a bit fey. Anyway, she saw me one night when I called at her house, and I knew that she had this reputation. She saw me, and it was partly her being led by me that they found my body. I was a Catholic priest as you can imagine. In fact, I didn't like the idea of being dead at all. I was very angry with myself for doing such a stupid thing. I know it sounds silly but it's amazing how even here you can be cross with yourself.

BG: What would be interesting to hear would be your reactions when you found that you weren't dead.

FOL: Well she was the only one who could see me, and she told everyone that she's seen me and therefore I must be dead.

BG: When did this actually take place, Father O'Leary?

FOL: It was just outside Cork and it must be well over a hundred years ago. It was quite a story for a long time. Of course, you would not be a Roman Catholic?

BG: No

FOL: I appreciate that you're a Spiritualist. Of course, for a long time I thought it was the Devil's work, but now I know different.

BG: And what are you doing now?

FOL: I'm teaching. Part of my work is to teach the children. I was always very attached to the children and when I was on your side. It was just a little country place and I used to take the children, and I used to give them lessons. In those days there was no proper school. Many of the children here have come here in infancy and they need care and help, and that's my main work.

BG: And I suppose you realize now that what you thought and believed was all wrong.

FOL: Well, I don't want to say things that are not true. I appreciate the fact that many of the things were supposition that I used to preach. But there is a fundamental truth in the teachings of the Christ. I know the Church has taken a powerful place and position which, if rightly used, could do a lot of good. At the same time a lot of the things that are preached are not true. I don't like to say things against the Church. That doesn't mean to say that I'm a pillar of the Church in any way, but at the same time I think it is good that even if some of the things that are taught are not quite right, that it is better to have a religion than no religion at all. But if I could come back, and if I could take over my work, I would certainly preach and I would certainly teach in a different way. I wouldn't preach in the narrow way in which I had become accustomed. But I think a man without a religion is not a good thing.

BG: But don't you think a religion can tie you, bind you?

FOL: Well, yes that's true. I know what you mean, but I think it is important to have a religion even though you may not be a good religious man, it is better to have a religion in your makeup and in your outlook and in your way of life than none at all. I expect you think I'm fencing with you.

BG: Well my way of looking at religion is the way you live, surely. It's not whether you're a Buddhist or a Spiritualist.

FOL: But you have to believe. You cannot be yourself a religious person unless you have a religious knowledge and experience.

BG: But believe WHAT?

FOL: I think it's very important to believe that there is a God. And that there is a Divine Power, call it what you like, and that we are responsible for our actions. If we are doing the wrong things and we cause unnecessary suffering to other people then we have to pay for our mistakes. I don't think it's a good thing to think that we can get away Scot free. I think people should be imbued with, well, not fear, as such, but that they should be responsible for their actions, and that they should think right in accordance with the will of God.

BG: In other words the karmic law.

FOL: You can put it like that. More than that, I think that we have to accept the fact (I don't say that I have seen God, it would be quite wrong to say that I have seen God because I have not seen God) but I believe there is a Supreme Force, something which we cannot understand, and which is the pivot around which we all live and have our being and revolve around. I think so many people put God out of their mind. They have no sense of responsibility for their thoughts and actions, and they have no fear of consequences. I think it's very bad. I think it's very necessary to have religious teaching.

BG: Are you still on the same old line of Heaven and Hell? You're not are you?

FOL: Not in the sense of Heaven and Hell in the accepted sense, but I think there is a kind of hell of remorse. A state in which they have to work out their own salvation. I don't say there's hell in the way of damnation and fire and all that. But at the same time I think we should realize that if there is good, which we know there is, and there is a good place, then there is also the opposite which is not good. It seems that you cannot hope to appreciate good unless you can know and understand evil. I'm not suggesting that one should be in any way bad, but it seems that these things that face one in life, they are there as a challenge, and we must face up to them, and we must fight them and we must work out our own salvation by resisting evil.

BG: The Roman Catholics teach, don't they, that the more you suffer, the better it will be when you die. Don't you think that's rather wrong?

FOL: I know how you feel. I am not suggesting that suffering is a good thing and I am not suggesting that it should be, we only know that it is, and from suffering we learn, and we learn many things which we can only learn through suffering. I think we have to face the fact that suffering is a reality, and that although we may do good and think good, it doesn't alter the fact that quite often we have to suffer. Christ had to suffer. All the disciples and saints had to suffer. They never found the path of righteousness and good easy. I think it is essential, whether we like it or not, and none of us like suffering, I do not see how we can appreciate anything that is good unless we go through a stage of evolution, and suffering is part of that evolution.

BG: Father O'Leary, I'm sorry I can't agree with you there. We all have to suffer, I know. But to deliberately let people suffer. And tell them that it will be all right when he goes over.

FOL: I think we are talking at cross purposes because I would not like you to think that I get any pleasure from people's suffering in that sense. I am not responsible for what other people think or what Catholics think, and I must admit that although I was a Catholic I have changed considerably in my outlook and my ideas. I do not go all the way with the Catholics anymore. Now I think differently but I think we must see that until man evolves, and this is going to take untold centuries of time, from what one has seen in the past the future isn't very promising in regards to man's progress because it seems to me that the more man progresses materially the less spiritual he becomes. But one has a ray of hope that man will progress and that suffering will be outlawed.

BG: Well it stands to reason that some of these flaws stem from a previous existence.

FOL: Well that may be true, I don't know about this reincarnation. I have no desire myself to come back to your world to live. There are a lot of very foolish people here which I've met on different spheres who are waiting and congregating together in great multitudes waiting to be resurrected in the physical body on earth. I don't belong to that category. I have sympathy for all human beings, but it strikes me that they are being very stupid to say the least.

BG: What I'm talking about is we are progressing from the imperfection to the perfection. You come up from other spheres..."

FOL: (interrupting) Well my dear, what is perfection? I don't think that we could ever reach a state of perfecting and quite frankly I don't think that we should want to. Once you reached that stage there would be nothing left to strive for and one would wonder what there is in eternity, what point? The point is there are always new things to experience, new things to learn. I am extremely happy in my own environment and I am doing good work with the children. I don't profess to know all the answers. I have not reached myself a very high stage of evolution.

BG: Don't you wish with the knowledge that you have now, don't you wish that you had known it in your existence on earth?

FOL: I do, I do. But I don't know how I would have been able to introduce it into my work, because it would have been forbidden by the Church.

BG: That's my point you see. Religion, it's so narrow, it's so confining.

FOL: I can appreciate that. I suppose that if I had known of this it would have meant that I would have had to have left the Church. It would not be tolerated by preaching what you call Spiritualism. I would have had to tone it down. It would be difficult and yet the whole history of the Church is full of these things.

BG: The Church has let people down, you see.

FOL: Well I want you to know that I am not here for idle talk. I have come here because I would like to be of some service, and I am very interested in all this, but I wish it was in the Church and not outside it.

BG: Well I'm glad it is outside the Church because if it were inside the Church it would be killed.

FOL: No, I think if it were inside the Church and properly presented, that this business of sitting in back rooms and singing these atrocious songs where I have been to some of these so-called meetings... I have listened to them singing some vile things which have nothing to do with spiritual matters whatsoever. In fact, I know that it is conducive to bad influences and I've seen all sorts of spirits manifesting there, and I think it's very dangerous. I think it should be within the Church and not outside it.

BG: The Church has tried to kill it. The Church is very frightened of it, you see.

FOL: The Church has every reason to be frightened of it because there are some very bad influences at work around the earth. One has to be very careful. If it was held within the Church in a spiritual way and had the Church's blessing then it would be a good thing.

BG: But the Church wants all the power.

FOL: I am here to help you because I know that you are anxious to work in a spiritual way. You are one of the few people I have met outside the Church that is at least approaching the subject in the right way. Anyway, this is a time of peace and goodwill. May the New Year bring you and your friend great happiness in the work that you do. I do know that you are doing a sincere work and that you are not frivolous like so many of these others. I must admit that I do not believe any more a lot of the things that I used to accept without even thinking about it. There are a lot of things that could be changed. I know there are many things which cause concern, and concerned me very much when I was on your side. We must be good friends, and I will come and speak to you again when I can. I must go. May the peace of God be with you. Goodbye.

This recording brings to mind the case of Father Messina in Boston. When Betty Greene asks Father O'Leary, "Don't you wish with the knowledge that you have now, don't you wish that you had known it in your existence on earth?", we could equally ask since Father Messina DOES have this knowledge while he is still on the earth, why doesn't he do something with it? Because, just like Father O'Leary, he would have to leave the Church. I do not believe that Father Richard Messina is an isolated case by any means. There are plenty of people in the Church, both priests and bishops, who have the knowledge of these things and yet, just the same, these things will never be revealed.

If, as the people who are on the other side tell us, the earth is the training ground, then it is inevitable that people will make mistakes. No one is so good or so bad that a pre-fixed eternity awaits them when they die as many Christians believe. Elizabeth Fry was a nineteenth-century prison reformer who came through on numerous occasions to speak to George Woods and Betty Greene. Fry was a major driving force behind new legislation to make the treatment of prisoners more humane, and she was supported in her efforts by the reigning monarch. Since 2001, she has been depicted on the Bank of England five pound note. Elizabeth Fry also helped the homeless, establishing a "nightly shelter" in London after seeing the body of a young boy in the winter of 1819/1820. In 1824, during a visit to Brighton, she instituted the Brighton District Visiting Society. The society arranged for volunteers to visit the homes of the poor and provide help and comfort to them. The plan was successful and was duplicated in other districts and towns across Britain. In a sitting on August 6, 1965 she had some definite thoughts about religious pronouncements:

Anyone with any scrap of intelligence who really seeks into the truths of the Bible ... and these truths are staring one fully in the face ... and yet so many people cannot see them. For instance, Christ Himself had no intention ... no desire to found any religious organization. This is completely and absolutely a man-made thing, which over the centuries has misled mankind. If you analyse the whole of Christ's teachings you will find that he was the most humble of souls, that he had no desire to form any kind of a religious organization. I think people will only begin to realize what Christ really was when they begin to discard a lot of outworn creeds and dogmas tacked on over the centuries by men who desired power and position.

Elizabeth Fry was more optimistic than many in saying that the "truths of the Bible" were staring one fully in the face. Most of orthodox Christianity has nothing to depend upon but the words of the Bible, a book written by, and heavily edited by, men.

Archie Matson, in his book *Afterlife*, concludes that much of the erroneous thinking about heaven and hell comes from the ideas laid down by the Christian Bible. Says Matson, "The Bible itself, and its various interpretations which have become part of traditional theology, form the biggest religious obstacle to the study and understanding of life beyond death."

One communicator who spoke to Woods and Greene about the Bible and religious teaching was Mike Fearon. Fearon was a soldier who was killed in the battle of Normandy. Unlike many others who were completely unknown, at least by voice, to the two researchers, Fearon's voice was soon identified by his mother.

Michael Fearon made his first appearance in 1947 when Woods and Greene were using a wire recorder. He told Woods he had been a biology teacher at Taunton School just before the war, and had been killed in the battle of Normandy in 1944, two weeks after D-Day. This was easy to check. Woods tracked down Fearon's mother and took her with him to Flint. The voice came through again. Mrs. Fearon announced it was her son and became a regular sitter in Flint's circle.

Extracts from two different sittings produced a volume of information from Fearon about life after death. Here is part of it, from a séance in December 1950, when the sitters were George Woods, Betty Greene and Fearon's mother:

M.F: It would make such a vast difference if people would realize that death isn't what they think it is. It's only an illusion. Man has created death in his own mind. It really doesn't exist. Man has always looked upon life as something purely materialistic, and when they started creating an idea of a new life, in their own minds, a new heaven, or new existence ... call it what you will ... they assumed that it would be in a physical body. Even today untold thousands of people that believe in a life after death ... their conception of it is extraordinarily materialistic.

Many, many people whom the world calls religious, because they conform to creeds and dogmas, think they're coming back upon the earth in a material form on the great day. Really, when you come to think about it, the things that some people believe are quite fantastic. And yet it's all man-made. There's not a scrap of evidence to support their theories, and the Church still preaches this ridiculous idea of heaven and hell. Heaven if you've been awfully good and you've followed certain tenets and so on, and hell if you haven't followed what they think is right. Really, when one comes to analyse it, it doesn't hold water at all.

Where have such absurd ideas come from in the first place? How did they creep into the Bible, and why have people found it so difficult, as Ellen Terry remarked, to ... "Discard a lot of outworn creeds and dogmas, tacked on over the centuries." The answer is a complicated one, but for me it is beginning to emerge after meeting and talking with people such as Father Messina. I cannot help but think that people make great efforts to avoid having to confront any new evidence that would force them to alter their preconceptions. I find it strange that the milieu of non-thinking church-going people in the United States have no conception of the psychic structure on which the Christian faith is built.

Alson J. Smith, in his book *Immortality: The Scientific Evidence,* writes, "The Church is based squarely on a psychic phenomena, the resurrection of Jesus. Without that great, paranormal event in history there would be no Christian Church. And buttressing that foundation are a whole series of psychic phenomena – healings, stigmata, miracles, etc." Smith adds, "The lost life of the Church can only be restored through a verification, by science through experiment, of the psychic phenomena on which the Church was originally built."

One of my more interesting experiences during my time as an Episcopalian was the reaction I got from my parish priest when I told him I was interested in psychical research and parapsychology. I was told to stay away from such subjects under pain of sin. Anglicanism is one of the few branches of Christianity that seems to walk a middle road between belief and non-belief. But as Bishop Pike said, "More belief, fewer beliefs!" How true.

James Harvey Hyslop was a professor of philosophy at Columbia University, a slight man with a neat brown beard, chilly grey eyes, and the faint pallor of ill health, which had dogged him since childhood. The look of fragility was deceptive; he possessed the combative temperament of a pit bull terrier.

Born in 1850, Hyslop came from an Ohio farm family. He grew up in the tiny community of Xenia, a swatch of fiercely tended fields surrounded by forest. His childhood had been one of farm labour, from caring for horses to breaking away corn stalks after a winter frost, and ultraconservative Christianity.

His parents belonged to a fundamentalist Presbyterian church and followed its teachings to the letter. The children were required to study the Bible daily, although during the week they could also read certain newspapers and books. On Sunday, the whole family spent six hours attending sermons and memorizing Psalms. "We were not allowed to play at games, swing or whistle, ride or walk for pleasure, pluck fruit from trees, black our shoes or read any secular literature," Hyslop recalled. He'd followed those teachings faithfully as a child, but as a university student majoring in philosophy, Hyslop became convinced that his father's faith was at odds with reality. The son still accepted the notion of a deity. It was the teaching of Christianity that now seemed to him preposterous, the impossibly simple explanation of creation, the egocentric notion of a chosen people, even the arguments for the divinity of Christ, seemed to Hyslop "fatally weak".

Determined not to be a hypocrite, he'd told his parents of his new perspective, proving to his father that, as suspected, a university education led to godlessness. In the following years, Hyslop's father alternated between ignoring his son and bombarding him with warnings of damnation. Even after Hyslop received his Ph.D in philosophy from Johns Hopkins, even after he was hired in 1889 as a professor of ethics and logic at Columbia, he knew full well that in his father's eyes he was a failure.

Hyslop fretted that he would never be able to repair the relationship, a loss made even more painful when his father died of throat cancer in 1896. He began to wonder about survival after death, whether his father lived on in some form, whether he could reach him yet.

In early 1898, after reading Richard Hodgson's endorsement of Mrs Piper, Hyslop realized that he had found the medium through whom he could pose his questions. He wrote to Hodgson asking for a series of sittings designed to challenge Mrs Piper's vaunted talents, and perhaps to resolve his personal dilemma. He proposed to make the challenge as difficult as he could. If it was too easy it would convince no one, including himself.

As they arranged it, Hyslop not only attended the sittings

anonymously, he wore a black mask over his face. He came masked even though he routinely waited outside a window until Mrs Piper was in full trance and Hodgson could gesture him into the room. Hodgson added another layer of protection to protect Hyslop's anonymity, a code name. Hodgson would refer to Hyslop only as "four times friend", since he had requested four sittings.

It was at the second sitting that Mrs Piper told him that a spirit was newly arrived in the room, and that the visitor's name was Robert Hyslop. As Hyslop told Hodgson afterward, he didn't think four sittings were going to be enough.

Michael Grosso, writing in *The Final Choice: Playing the Survival Game*, says on this subject:

> Liberal Christianity has so far shown little interest in using psychical research in its effort to reconcile ancient faith with modern rationality. The liberal theologians have demythologized Christianity. Yet it was the belief in the supernatural, the living mythology of the resurrection, and the reality of the miraculous, that inspired the primitive Christian communities.

Mike Fearon shed some additional light on how many of the absurd ideas about life after death affect people in the afterlife. The following is taken from a 1952 sitting with George Woods, Betty Greene and Fearon's mother:

> M.F: In fact, some people coming here believing that they were really God's elect, that they were the chosen ones still exist over here in a certain sphere, believing that they are the only persons who exist in this world. They are blind to any other form of life or advancement. They genuinely think that they are the only ones over here, and even they are waiting to come back on earth in a physical shape, waiting for the

resurrection of the body. All these false teachings that the Church has given over the centuries have done untold harm to untold millions of people.

Woods: What happens, Mike, to people who are so bound to creeds and dogmas when they pass over to the other side?

MF: A man immediately after death is no different to what he was five minutes before. That is in regard to his outlook, his character and his personality. And therefore a person who has very strong religious convictions still holds them very strongly when he comes here. But he begins to realize that he's rather like a fish out of water, that a lot of his old ideas and teachings just don't apply, they don't fit.

The first thing he realizes here is that everything is normal. Everything is natural. People are very much the same as they were on earth, but without all the heaviness of the material life. He begins to realize that many of the old ideas he had were purely material conceptions of heaven and God. He begins to realize that life here is a normal, natural thing, and that he himself is exactly as he was. But much that he had held fast to and which he thought would, shall we say, make for himself a heaven because of his beliefs, he finds is not necessarily so, that many, many phases of life exist, and that he must adjust himself to his condition in which he finds himself.

And of course, there are always those who will meet him ... friends and relations ... people he's known and loved and who still love him, and they will talk to him and endeavour to make him realize that he has to rid himself of much that he thought was true when on earth, and make himself mentally free to be able to adjust to his new form of existence.

So many people have such a hazy idea of what life is like on this side, and those that have very strong orthodox views ... they really do believe that they are elected for a life which is far superior to any other, which of course is not true.

Did Fearon exaggerate? Nine years later, a voice came through claiming to be just such a person as Fearon had described. The man was George Briggs, and he explained to Woods and Greene how he had trod the long, difficult path out of the darkness of his own thinking into the light:

> My name is Briggs. I was for many years, when on your side, a member of the Christadelphians. This is an American sect believing that they, and hardly anyone else, will be raised from the dead and return to earth when Christ returned to subdue the world from Jerusalem.

Having never heard of the Christadephians myself, I decided to do some research. Christadelphians believe that people are separated from God because of their sins but that mankind can be reconciled to him by becoming disciples of Jesus Christ. This is by belief in the gospel, through repentance, and through baptism by total immersion in water. They do not believe we can be sure of being saved, believing instead that salvation comes as a result of a life of obedience to the commands of Christ. After death, believers are in a state of non-existence, knowing nothing until the Resurrection at the return of Christ. Following the judgement at that time, the accepted receive the gift of immortality, and live with Christ on a restored Earth, assisting him to establish the Kingdom of God and to rule over the mortal population for a thousand years (the Millennium). Christadelphians believe that the Kingdom will be centred upon Israel, but Jesus Christ will also reign over all the other nations on the earth.

Briggs' continued:

> In my own narrow way, when I was on your side, I sincerely believed that only those who accepted and believed as I did would inherit the Kingdom of God. I know this is a fallacy *now*, and that *all* peoples inherit the kingdom of God because

it is a natural law. When a man dies his spirit inherits the spiritual realms which are all around and about your earth world. It is inescapable.

There is no one left out, and man inherits according to his nature and his achievement, or lack of achievement, going to a lesser condition or place. In other words man receives exactly what he himself has created in his life, his outlook and his way of life. Religion cannot make a man a better person. This is something that can only come when man realizes that he is already in embryo a spiritual being.

My mind was closed to truth. When I first came here, I found myself in an environment which for me was very satisfactory and very happy. I was in paradise. But I realize now that I was in a fool's paradise, a condition of life which consisted entirely of people of like mind, people who had believed as I had believed, who had accepted as I had accepted what I thought was the complete and absolute truth. We were content with our meetings, and our singing of hymns and our prayers, and we would talk often of the time when we should be brought back to earth to be resurrected as we had been told, and that there would be a great resurrection day and we would all be gathered up together and we would enter into our physical bodies and become earthly people living in an earthly paradise.

But I was fortunate, because gradually I began to feel within myself a little uneasy. I cannot explain how this first came about. In some strange way I began to feel that there was something that was not quite as it should be. I began to wonder if there were other worlds apart from the one in which I was existing. Gradually I became conscious of other beings who were not of our sect, who were not our persuasion. And these beings became not only apparent to me as visions, but as real people. And I became conscious of their thoughts. It was as if they were not speaking, and yet I could hear within myself what they were trying to convey to me. Eventually I was asked to make the experiment to go on a trip. And so I went with one particular soul who seemed to be the leader of the group whose name was Bernard. He told me as we made our way through many places that he, when on earth, had been a Roman Catholic priest. This immediately caused me great concern. In our particular religious body we always looked upon the Catholics as the devil's own children. He explained to me that he had been a Catholic the same as I had been of my own faith, and that we were both wrong. We both had very strong views which were far from the truth. He said that we should forget what we were, but rather be concerned with what we might be.

Their journey took them through cities and small communities; they observed different cultures, different races. The journey ended in a beautiful city where everyone seemed to be full of love:

There is no barrier to man once his mind is unshackled, once he is free to think for himself. So many have to go through varying degrees and conditions of life before they reach that stage of illumination.

Some people seem to bypass all the creeds and dogmas when on earth, and walk a simple, straightforward spiritual path. Carl Jung, who we met in the first chapter, was one of those. It slowly has become clear to me Dr. Jung's purpose in his meeting with me when I was sixteen in that materialization séance. We are cut from the same cloth so to speak. There is not a day in my life when I do not think back on that strange and yet wonderful meeting so long ago. I wish I had known him in life. I feel the same way about Jim Pike. He, also, died too soon.

Writing in *Memories, Dreams, Reflections*, Jung says:

During my student days I received much stimulation in regard to religious questions. At home I had the welcome opportunity to talk with a theologian who had been my father's vicar. He was distinguished not only by his phenomenal appetite, which put mine quite in the shade, but by his remarkable erudition. From him I learned a great deal about the Church Fathers and the history of dogma. He also introduced me to new aspects of Protestant theology. Ritschl's theology was much in fashion in those days. Its historicism irritated me, especially the comparison with a railway train. Ritschl compared Christ's coming to the shunting of a railway train. The engine gives a push from behind, the motion passes through the entire train, and the foremost car begins to move. Thus the impulse given by Christ is transmitted down the centuries. The theological students with whom I had discussions in the fraternity all seemed quite content with the theology of the historical effect produced by Christ's life. This view seemed to me not only soft-witted but altogether lifeless. Neither could I subscribe to the tendency to move Christ into the foreground and make him the sole decisive figure in the drama of God and man. To me this absolutely belied Christ's own view that the Holy Ghost, who had begotten him, would take his place among men after his death. For me the Holy Ghost was a manifestation of the inconceivable God. The workings of the Holy Ghost were not only sublime but also partook of that strange and even questionable quality which characterized the deeds of Yahweh, whom I naively identified with the Christian image of God as I had been taught in my instruction for confirmation. (I was also not aware at this time that the devil, properly speaking, had been born with Christianity.) Lord Jesus was to me unquestionably a man and therefore a fallible figure, or else a mere mouthpiece of the Holy Ghost. This highly unorthodox view, a far cry from the theological one, naturally ran up against utter incomprehension. The disappointment I felt about this gradually led me to a kind of resigned indifference, and confirmed my conviction that in religious matters only experience counted.

My friend Alex Tanous also had similar struggles with his religion in his early years. During the summers of 1988 and 1989 I visited Maine regularly and we often had long talks about his conflict between his psychic powers and his religion. In his early years Alex often told me about his ghost investigations and about seeing ghosts and spirits of dead people. "I was told that the only ghost was the Holy Ghost," Alex revealed one day as we sat out by the swimming pool:

> My parents feared that my psychic powers would get me into trouble. Though we were respected members of the community, our Lebanese background, the fact that we belonged to the Maronite Rite (an Eastern Rite Catholic, rather than the Roman Rite Catholic) and my father's reputation for readings had already put distance between us and our fellow townsfolk. Now, my mother feared that if I also became known as a psychic, we might become outcast – at the moment we needed goodwill from the community more than ever.

Alex's problems, far from disappearing when he grew up, seemed to get worse:

> Soon, I entered high school; things took a turn for the worse for me there. I attended a public school, where some of the teachers were priests. It wasn't long before I was listening to lectures on moral theology. And as I listened, a chill came over my heart.

According to Church doctrine, whenever I practised my psychic powers, I was in sin, I was doing evil. If I continued my ways, I was sure to be condemned to hell. Yet it was my nature to be psychic. I could no more turn off the flow of premonitions and psychic images than I could stop breathing.

No priest ever actually told me that I was evil (at least not during my high school days). In fact, one went out of his way to tell me I wasn't, that I was only "a hundred years ahead of my time". But I heard many priests say that the kinds of things I was doing were evil. And when I read their cannon law, there was no doubt in my mind that I was committing a sin whenever I had a paranormal experience.

After a while, I began to feel I was the carrier of some sort of plague. I could find no way to honour my religion, take my place in the community, and still be true to myself. Faced with this insoluble problem, I slowly began to withdraw into myself. I became more and more introverted.

Three people, all from the twentieth century, all were ahead of their time, Carl Jung, Jim Pike, and Alex Tanous. And perhaps I should add my own name to the list.

One religious leader who helped open a few doors and let in some fresh air, after his life on earth was finished, was Dean Inge of St. Paul's Cathedral, who announced himself at a Woods and Greene sitting in 1965:

It is an appalling thought (he began) that the teachings of Christ, the fundamental truths that he and other great souls have taught, have been obscured beyond belief ...

This man Jesus who came into the world in such a humble way and lived a life giving forth a realization of God's will and purpose endeavoured to show that the only way to development of spiritual consciousness was through service and love ... through putting one's self further and further into the background. In other words, become a vessel for greater souls, for greater teachings. We are instruments and when we realize how much we can give out, which so few ever do, then we begin to grow and expand, and then we begin to become at least something like Christ. But when we think that one person, even though sent from the highest, can save us, it is a fallacy.

If Christ were to return to Earth today, you wouldn't have anything to do with him, in spite of all that the Church teaches. The Churches themselves probably would be the first to crucify him again if they could. Why? Because they do not like those who come with a message such as this ...

Christ is found in the hearts of all men whose minds are open and sincere and anxious to understand and to see. Until man can strip himself of preconceived ideas and shake from himself the old beliefs, until he can realize that he is within himself able to tune into the highest, he will not find truth.

When man leaves your world he has to unlearn many things as I did (Inge concluded). There are many here with me who feel as I do, that if we could come back with our present knowledge how different we would think and act, and how different we would speak.

Inge, like Cosmo Lang, had found that things were vastly different from the way he had pictured them during his clerical role on earth. Though both had been suspicious that there was more than a germ of truth in communication with discarnate entities, Lang suppressed the findings of the committee – not because he didn't accept the evidence but because he was afraid it could undermine the Church, and probably even destroy it.

If the day ever comes when religious leaders can overcome their own fears, like those of Father Messina, of becoming an outcast, then it may be possible to have a revolution in religious thinking.

I agree with Christopher Hitchens in his book, *God Is Not Great* when he says:

Religion has run out of justifications. Thanks to the telescope and the microscope, it no longer offers an explanation of anything important. Where once it used to be able, by its total command of a world-view, to prevent the emergence of rivals, it can now only impede and retard – or try to turn back – the measurable advances that we have made. Sometimes, true, it will artfully concede them. But this is to offer itself the choice between irrelevance and obstruction, impotence or outright reaction, and, given this choice, it is programmed to select the worse of the two.

I long for the day when religion no longer exists.

The taboo our culture has imposed on the whole subject of death can be removed.

And in the words of George Meek, "Something else that can be jettisoned is the accumulated non-productive religious dogma that has ruined countless lives over the centuries to the extent that it has imposed burdens of fear and guilt."

Chapter Five

The Stars Impel

It is my belief, which I cannot prove here, that within each of us is a creative core that actively creates the universe, either by making up each part out of nothing or by agreeing in advance, prior to our physical incarnation, to play a certain game with certain rules. In this scheme your horoscope becomes a symbol of your intentions.
Robert Hand, *Planets in Transit*

Cassius:
The fault, dear Brutus, is not in our stars, But in ourselves, that we are underlings.
Julius Caesar (I, ii, 140-141)

I began the study of astrology in 1970 in Virginia Beach, Virginia, with a teacher by the name of Ray Williams (no relation). Ray taught me the basics of astrology and started me on a path of discovery that would last the rest of my life. Ray was also a Theosophist and his class was saturated with tales of "the Masters". Madame Blavatsky, Alice Bailey and others in the theosophical movement. He was one of those astrologers who believed in karma and reincarnation and read the chart from that point of view. I remember Ray putting his own chart up on the blackboard and illustrating why he seemingly was not able to make money.

When I discuss my experiences with astrology in this chapter, I am not talking about the usual sort of astrology depicted in the daily newspapers by the late Jean Dixon, or in Linda Goodman's book, *Sun Signs*. I am talking about the total study of astrology which rightly includes planets, house placement and aspects.

Astrology has been dated to at least the 2nd millennium BCE, with roots in calendrical systems used to predict seasonal shifts and to interpret celestial cycles as signs of divine communications. A form of astrology was practised in the first dynasty of Mesopotamia (1950–1651 BCE). Chinese astrology was elaborated in the Zhou dynasty (1046–256 BCE). Hellenistic astrology after 332 BCE mixed Babylonian astrology with Egyptian Decanic astrology in Alexandria, creating horoscopic astrology. Alexander the Great's conquest of Asia allowed astrology to spread to Ancient Greece and Rome. In Rome, astrology was associated with 'Chaldean wisdom'. In the seventh century CE, astrology was taken up by Islamic scholars, and Hellenistic texts were translated into Arabic and Persian. In the twelfth century, Arabic texts were imported to Europe and translated into Latin. Major astronomers including Tycho Brahe, Johannes Kepler and Galileo practised as court astrologers. Astrological references appear in literature in the works of poets such as Dante Alighieri and Geoffrey Chaucer, and of playwrights such as Christopher Marlowe and William Shakespeare. Throughout most of its history, astrology was considered a scholarly tradition. It was accepted in political and academic contexts, and was connected with other studies, such as astronomy, alchemy, meteorology, and medicine. Astrology, in its broadest sense, is the search for meaning in the sky. Early evidence for humans making conscious attempts to measure, record, and predict seasonal changes by reference to astronomical cycles, appears as markings on bones and cave walls, which show that lunar cycles were being noted as early as 25,000 years ago. This was a first step towards recording the Moon's influence upon tides and rivers, and towards organising a communal calendar. Farmers addressed agricultural needs with increasing knowledge of the constellations that appear in the different seasons – and used the rising of particular star-groups to herald annual floods or seasonal activities. By the third millennium BCE, civilisations had sophisticated awareness of celestial cycles, and may have oriented temples in alignment with heliacal risings of the stars.

Scattered evidence suggests that the oldest known astrological references are copies of texts made in the ancient world. The Venus tablet of Ammisaduqa is thought to have been compiled in Babylon around 1700 BCE. A scroll documenting an early use of electional astrology is doubtfully ascribed to the reign of the Sumerian ruler Gudea of Lagash (c. 2144–2124 BCE). This describes how the gods revealed to him in a dream the constellations that would be most favourable for the planned construction of a temple. However, there is controversy about whether these were genuinely recorded at the time or merely ascribed to ancient rulers by posterity. The oldest undisputed evidence of the use of astrology as an integrated system of knowledge is therefore attributed to the records of the first dynasty of Mesopotamia (1950–1651 BCE). This astrology had some parallels with Hellenistic Greek (western) astrology, including the zodiac, a norming point near 9 degrees in Aries, the trine aspect, planetary exaltations, and the dodekatemoria (the twelve divisions of 30 degrees each). The Babylonians viewed celestial events as possible signs rather than as causes of physical events.

Western astrology is a form of divination based on the construction of a horoscope for an exact moment, such as a person's birth. It uses the tropical zodiac, which is aligned to the equinoctial points.

Western astrology is founded on the movements and relative positions of celestial bodies such as the Sun, Moon and planets, which are analysed by their movement through signs of the zodiac (twelve spatial divisions of the ecliptic) and by their aspects (based on geometric angles) relative to one another. They are also considered by their placement in houses (twelve spatial divisions of the sky). Astrology's modern representation in western popular media is usually reduced to sun sign astrology, which considers only the zodiac sign of the Sun at an individual's date of birth, and represents only one twelfth of the total chart.

The horoscope visually expresses the set of relationships for the time and place of the chosen event. These relationships are between the seven 'planets', signifying tendencies such as war and love; the twelve signs of the zodiac; and the twelve houses. Each planet is in a particular sign and a particular house at the chosen time, when observed from the chosen place, creating two kinds of relationship. A third kind is the aspect of each planet to every other planet, where for example two planets 120° apart (in 'trine') are in a harmonious relationship, but two planets 90° apart ('square') are in a conflicted relationship. Together these relationships and their interpretations supposedly form "the language of the heavens".

My early beginnings and interest in astrology stemmed from my study of the Edgar Cayce readings at the Association for Research and Enlightenment, also in Virginia Beach. Cayce was another one of my early heroes and his headquarters were only a mile or two from my home. In his several thousand life readings, some of which I studied in depth, Cayce continually referred to astrology and to the astrological portents of the people he was reading for.

I will never forget my first trip to the A.R.E, as it is called. Situated across the street from the Atlantic Ocean on Atlantic Avenue, sits an imposing building that was put up in the 1970s to house the library of readings which are now on microfilm. It also houses an enormous library of psychic and occult books, with over five hundred on astrology alone.

Cayce was not born in Virginia Beach. He came there from Kentucky. Edgar Cayce was born on March 18, 1877, near Beverly, south of Hopkinsville, Kentucky. He was one of six children of farmers Leslie B. Cayce and Carrie Cayce. A very spiritual child, he played with the 'little folk' and sometimes 'saw' his deceased grandfather. He regarded them all as incorporeal because he could see through them if he looked hard enough. However, he found it very difficult to keep his mind on his lessons at school.

He was taken to church when he was 10, and from then on he read the Bible, becoming engrossed, and completing a dozen readings by the time he was 12. In May 1889, while reading the Bible in his hut in the woods, he 'saw' a woman with wings who told him that his prayers were answered, and asked him what he wanted most of all. He was frightened, but he said that most of all he wanted to be helpful to others, especially sick children. He decided he would like to be a missionary.

The next night, after a complaint from the school teacher, his father ruthlessly tested him for spelling, eventually knocking him out of his chair with exasperation. At that point, Edgar 'heard' the voice of the lady who had appeared yesterday. She told him that if he could sleep a little 'they' could help him. He begged for a rest and put his head on the spelling book. When his father came back into the room and woke him up, he knew all the answers. In fact, he could repeat anything in the book. His father thought he had been fooling before and knocked him out of the chair again. Eventually, Edgar used all his school books that way.

By 1892, the teacher regarded Edgar as his best student. On being questioned, Edgar told the teacher that he saw pictures of the pages in the books. His father became proud of this accomplishment and spread it around, resulting in Edgar becoming 'different' from his peers.

Shortly after this, Edgar exhibited an ability to diagnose in his sleep. He got struck on the base of the spine by a ball in a school game, after which he began to act very strangely, and eventually was put to bed. He went to sleep and diagnosed the cure, which his family prepared and which cured him as he slept. His father boasted that his son was, "the greatest fellow in the world when he's asleep". However, this ability was not demonstrated again for several years.

Cayce's uncommon personality is also shown by an unusual incident in which he rode a certain mule back to the farmhouse at the end of a work day. This stunned everyone there, as the mule could not be ridden. The owner, thinking it may be time to break the animal in again, attempted to mount it but was immediately thrown off. Cayce left for his family in the city that evening.

In December 1893, the Cayce family moved to Hopkinsville, Kentucky, and occupied 705 West Seventh on the southeast corner of Seventh and Young Streets. During this time, Cayce received an eighth-grade education, he is said by the Association for Research and Enlightenment to have developed psychic abilities, and left the family farm to pursue various forms of employment.

Cayce's education stopped in the ninth grade because his family could not afford the costs involved. (A ninth-grade education was often considered more than sufficient for working-class children.) Much of the remainder of Cayce's younger years would be characterized by a search for both employment and money.

Throughout his life, Cayce was drawn to church as a member of the Disciples of Christ. He read the Bible once a year every year, taught at Sunday school, and recruited missionaries. He said he could see auras around people, spoke to angels, and heard voices of departed relatives. In his early years, he agonized over whether these psychic abilities were spiritually delivered from the highest source.

In 1900, Cayce formed a business partnership with his father to sell Woodmen of the World Insurance; however, in March he was struck by severe laryngitis that resulted in a complete loss of speech. Unable to work, he lived at home with his parents for almost a year. He then decided to take up the trade of photography, an occupation that would exert less strain on his voice. He began an apprenticeship at the photography studio of W.R. Bowles in Hopkinsville, and eventually became quite talented in his trade.

In 1901, a travelling stage hypnotist and entertainer named Hart, who referred to himself as "The Laugh Man" was performing at the Hopkinsville Opera House. Hart heard about Cayce's condition and offered to attempt a cure. Cayce accepted his offer, and the experiment was conducted in the office of Dr. Manning Brown, the local throat specialist. Cayce's voice allegedly returned while in a hypnotic trance but disappeared on awakening. Hart tried a posthypnotic suggestion that the voice would continue to function after the trance, but this proved unsuccessful.

Hart had appointments at other cities, but admitted he had failed because Cayce would not go into the third stage of hypnosis to take a suggestion. A New York hypnotist, Dr Quackenboss, found the same impediment but, after returning to New York, suggested that Cayce should be prompted to take over his own case while in the second stage of hypnosis. The only local hypnotist, Al Layne, offered to help Cayce restore his voice. Layne suggested that Cayce describe the nature of his condition and cure while in a hypnotic trance. Cayce described his own ailment from a first-person plural point of view: "we" instead of the singular "I". In subsequent sessions, when Cayce wanted to indicate that the connection was made to the "entity" of the person that was requesting the reading, he would generally start off with, "We have the body." According to the reading for the "entity" of Cayce, his voice loss was due to psychological paralysis, and could be corrected by increasing the blood flow to the voice box. Layne suggested that the blood flow be increased and Cayce's face supposedly became flushed with blood, and both his chest and throat turned bright red. After 20 minutes, Cayce, still in a trance, declared the treatment over. On awakening, his voice was alleged to have remained normal. Apparently, relapses occurred, but were said to have been corrected by Layne in the same way, and eventually the cure was said to be permanent.

Layne had read of similar hypnotic cures by the Marquis de Puységur, a follower of Franz Mesmer, and was keen to explore the limits of the healing knowledge involved with the trance voice. He asked Cayce to describe Layne's own ailments and suggest cures, and reportedly found the results both accurate and effective. Layne suggested that Cayce offer his trance healing to the public. Cayce was reluctant, but he finally agreed, on the condition that readings would be free. He began, with Layne's help, to offer free treatments to the townspeople. Reports of Cayce's work appeared in the newspapers, which inspired many postal inquiries. Cayce stated he could work just as effectively using a letter from the individual as with the person being present in the room. Given only the person's name and location, Cayce said he could diagnose the physical and mental conditions of what he termed "the entity", and then provide a remedy. Cayce soon became famous, and people from around the world sought his advice through correspondence.

Cayce's mature period, in which he created the several institutions that would survive him, can be considered to have started in 1925. By this time he was a professional psychic with a small staff of employees and volunteers. The readings increasingly came to involve occult or esoteric themes.

In 1929 the Cayce hospital was established in Virginia Beach, sponsored by a Morton Blumenthall, a recipient of the trance readings. Blumenthall was a wealthy New York stockbroker who had the most extensive readings with Cayce, some 468. He is said to have made considerable gains through insights into the stock market's futures until it crashed that year. This event caused Blumenthall to withdraw his funding and the hospital eventually closed its doors shortly after.

The depression years saw Cayce turn his attention to spiritual teachings. In 1931, Edgar Cayce's friends and family asked him how they could become psychic like him. Out of this seemingly simple question came an eleven-year discourse that led to the creation of "Study Groups". From his altered state, Cayce relayed to this group that the purpose of life is not to become psychic, but to become a more spiritually aware and loving person. Study Group #1 was told that they could "bring light to a waiting world" and that these lessons would still be studied a hundred years into the future. The readings were now about dreams, coincidence (synchronicity), developing intuition, karma, the akashic records, astrology, past-life relationships, soul mates and other esoteric subjects. Hundreds of books have been published about these readings.

Cayce gained national prominence in 1943 after the publication of a high-profile article in the magazine Coronet titled "Miracle Man of Virginia Beach". World War II was taking its toll on American soldiers and he felt he could not refuse the families who requested help for their loved ones that were missing in action. He increased the frequency of his readings to eight per day to try to make an impression on the ever-growing pile of requests. He said this took a toll on his health as it was emotionally draining and often fatigued him. The readings themselves scolded him for attempting too much and that he should limit his workload to just two life readings a day or else these good efforts would eventually kill him.

Edgar Cayce suffered a stroke at the age of 67, in September 1944, and died on January 3, 1945.

Cayce had a secretary, Gladys Davis Turner, who took notes of most of Cayce's readings. When I first went to the A.R.E she still had a parking place in the lot of the new building which had just been put up. I believe I must have devoured at least half of the books on astrology at the A.R.E library. I did most of the research for my book, *A Life Beyond Death* in that library. Astrology, for me, opened up a whole new world.

By the mid-1970s I was in Boston, working at public radio

and television station WGBII. It was while in Boston that I encountered another astrologer, Isabel Hickey. Isabel, known as "Issie", also taught astrology from the perspective of karma and reincarnation. She always remarked that a person's astrology chart was a reflection of that person's "spiritual bank book".

If Evangeline Adams was the Mother of Astrology in the first half of the twentieth century, Isabel Hickey filled that role for many of us who studied in the Sixties and the Seventies. She managed to be both esoteric and down to earth, never an easy juggling act.

For those of us who quaked at the fatalistic tone of the few other texts of the time like Charles E. O. Carter's *The Astrological Aspects*, Isabel's more Humanistic viewpoint brought both relief and hope. As one of her books said "It is all right", we can learn and evolve spiritually by studying astrology. These ideas are taken for granted now, so it is hard to imagine how groundbreaking they were for the time. Issie's Friday night class was dubbed the "Friday night fix".

I had been studying the writings of astrologer C.E. O. Carter, (Charles Ernest Owen Carter). Generally regarded as one of the masters of astrology during his lifetime, Carter's work, especially his insistence on first principles, remains a powerful influence on astrology and astrologers to this day. He is chiefly known as the co-founder and first principal of the London Faculty of Astrological Studies (indeed it was his idea).

He was born on 31 January 1887, at 11:01 p.m. GMT, in Parkstone, Poole, England. Carter began his career by graduating from the University of London in 1913 and practising as a barrister. He served in the army during the First World War and it was at this time he became interested in astrology after requesting one of Alan Leo's famous "one-shilling reports".

Besides co-founding the Faculty of Astrological Studies, Carter was the second President of the Astrological Lodge of the Theosophical Society from 1922 for many years. He also founded the Astrological Quarterly magazine in 1926 and was its Editor until 1959. As a final flourish, in 1955 Carter correctly predicted his own death would be in 1968. He died at age 81, on 4 October 1968 at 4:30 p.m. in London.

Having read and studied the books of both Carter and Hickey and having now spent forty years seeing astrology work in my life and the lives of others, I tend to agree with the more fatalistic view of Carter.

It is impossible to know how and why the motion of the planets seems to correspond to future events, but it does. I have seen it in my own life and I have seen it in the life of my clients who have come for readings. I am still a practising astrologer today and have no doubt whatsoever that in some strange way, which is impossible to understand, the plants influence our lives. One of the best ways to know when an upcoming event is likely to happen is by plotting out what is known as the transits to the natal planets.

Astrological transits are one of the main means used in horoscopic astrology to forecast future trends and developments (the other means used is astrological progression, which progresses the horoscope forward in time according to set methods). As its name implies, astrological transits involve a method of interpreting the ongoing movement of the planets as they transit the horoscope. This is most often done for the birth or Natal Chart of a particular individual. Particular attention is paid to changes of sign, or house, and to the aspects or angles the transiting planets make with the natal chart.

A particularly important transit is the planetary return. This occurs when a transiting planet returns to the same point in the sky that it occupied at the moment of a person's birth. What this means is that the planet has completed a whole circuit of the sky, and signifies that a new cycle in the person's life is beginning. The most significant returns are those of the outer planets Jupiter and Saturn. The Jupiter return occurs approximately every 12 years and heralds a new phase of growth and development. The Saturn return occurs approximately every 30 years, and heralds a new phase in the ageing process when new realities and responsibilities must be faced.

Most astrologers nowadays regard the term 'prediction' as something of a misnomer, as modern astrology does not claim to directly predict future events as such. Instead it is claimed that an astrological pattern with regard to the future can correspond with any one of a variety of possibilities. What is, in fact, foretold is the trend of circumstances and the nature of the individual's reaction to the situation. In other words, progressed and transiting movements of the planets indicate phases in the individual's life when the potential shown in the natal chart will be given opportunities for development, whether through favourable or unfavourable circumstances. I do not agree with this interpretation for several reasons. First, it does not tally with my experience as an astrologer. I have seen astrological transits forecast events that come true to the day. Second, I believe the term "free will" is overrated.

All modern astrologers stress the role of free will. It is asserted that astrology does not reveal fate or patterns which are 'written in stone', rather it reveals a person's strengths and weakness, talents and opportunities. The horoscope supposedly does not determine the future, but shows the possible paths that lie ahead so that the individual can choose between them. Modern astrologers argue that no planetary aspect brings a fate that cannot be counteracted in some way and some benefit derived from it – what actual events happen are largely dependent upon the freedom of choice of the individual. I simply do not agree with this. "The role of the astrologer is to create self-knowledge and awareness of the movement of the planets and their meaning, so as to give the individual an improved ability to make reasoned and sensible life choices", says one astrologer. If that were true, one might just as well consult a therapist. My experience as an astrologer demonstrates clearly that there is some mysterious force operating in the Universe which we can never hope to understand, and that force shapes our destiny. This is also the belief of astrologer Abbeygale Quinn, who I will discuss more fully in another chapter. Quinn also does not believe in free will and says so on her website. Some good examples of what I am talking about can be found in the transit of the planet Saturn over the tenth house cusp of my chart. This occurred in July 1996. I lost my job in radio in the exact week in which this transit occurred. President Nixon fell from power with this same aspect. Likewise, when transiting Pluto, which rules power struggles, made an opposition aspect to my natal Jupiter, I engaged in a power struggle with the management of a radio station over an issue which was important to me and resigned my job. Oddly enough, a Virginia Beach clairvoyant told me before I took the job that I would only be there seven months. I was there exactly seven months.

Transits of the inner planets (including sun and moon) are generally not considered by astrologers to be of major importance, as they are of such short duration, and so have a limited effect. Most astrologers would not chart these transits on an ongoing basis as they occur so frequently and are so fleeting in their operation. The following are their main characteristics:

Transiting Sun is at its peak for about two days and has an effect on health, energy and willpower in the area of life indicated by the natal planet, sign and house being transited. Greater creativity, activity and open expression.

Transiting Moon lasts a few hours at most and affects mainly moods and feelings, not always consciously, according to the planet, sign and house being transited.

Transiting Mercury is at its peak for only a day or two. A useful time to help with backlogs of correspondence, make short journeys or visits. Thought patterns and focus will be altered positively or negatively depending on the nature of the aspect and aspected planet. A good time to write letters, e-mail, make phone calls and generally communicate with others. Combined with Venus, a Mercury transit can indicate entertaining, or perhaps giving a talk or lecture. Mercury transits to natal sun and ascendant indicate a good time for making minor changes – buying, selling and exchanging things.

Transiting Venus is at its peak for about two days, and usually indicates enjoyment in your social life and feelings of love. Social behaviour will be altered. Sometimes the influence is financial through receiving gifts or money. Transits to the sun and ascendant indicate a good time to buy new clothes or to beautify yourself, and transits to the moon, a good time to beautify the home and buy new household goods. Transits to Mercury and Jupiter indicate a good time to entertain, and transits to its own place and to the midheaven, a good time to be entertained. Transits to Neptune are a good time to go to the cinema or theatre, while Uranus transits are favourable for taking chances in romance!

Transiting Mars energizes the areas of life related to the affected natal planet. The person will be more energetic and be able to work harder than usual. But Mars can also promote tension and anger, so there is a need to watch the temper during a Mars transit, especially for transits with the moon. Plan to keep busy during a Mars transit so as to have an outlet for this excessive energy. There is also a need to take extra precautions against rushing and accidents. Be on especial guard when Mars transits the sun or the ascendant.

Outer planets

The transits of the outer planets are considered to be the most important by astrologers, as their effects can last for up to several years. The following are their main characteristics.

Transiting Jupiter: Lasts some months and presents opportunities in the area of life involved by the aspected planet;

conducive to periods of expansion and exceptional opportunities for achieving success in business, receiving benefits, good favour. Travelling, knowledge and new experiences are possible. Difficult aspects may lead to serious misjudgements, exaggerated, extravagant behaviour and sheer bad luck.

Transiting Saturn can indicate periods of limitation, restriction, possible ill-health, depleted energy, losses, depressive moods, death, lack of co-operation, general misfortune. Respect and social status will be affected. Yet, can also be a useful time for wise long-term planning, conserving energy, building up resources, study, serious contemplation of life and self. Patience will be needed as this is not a time to push ahead with plans and affairs, and forcing matters will not do much good. It is better to accept that this aspect will slow down the rhythm of life in the house or planet involved showing which lessons of discipline and structure must be learned. A time to consolidate and prepare for more go-ahead indications in the chart.

Transiting Uranus: A period of unplanned, sudden drastic upheavals and changes can be expected, including a dramatic turn to circumstances, with a new way of life opening. Possible periods of inspiration, originality, creativeness, unconventional and rebellious behaviour. Greater desire for individuality, invention, expression and freedom, and new relationships are possible.

Transiting Neptune can indicate peculiar, strange, confusing and chaotic happenings, but also great creativity and inspiration. Neptune dissolves ideas and emotions in the house or planet which is aspected. Diffusion and idealization tends to occur and a tendency to fall into illusions or dreams. Spiritualization of the arena of life involved occurs, artistic practices, theatre, spiritual or religious experiences are possible at this time. Difficult aspects may stimulate neurotic, escapist, suicidal and mentally disturbed tendencies. Victimization, delusions, misunderstandings or saviour roles are possible at this time, and over-involvement with alcohol, drugs.

Transiting Pluto is conducive to periods of major transformation in the life-pattern. Often the end of a 'chapter of experience' for the start of another, due to eruptive developments that have been 'brewing up' under the surface for some time. Pluto will transform, renew and revolutionize the ideas or emotions in the house or the planet which is aspected. Deep psychological changes occur, cycles of either symbolic or real death and rebirth, obsessions, fateful encounters, power urges, power struggles and sexual issues. Old issues from past can come to surface. Pluto exposes these issues so that their nature may be understood and the subject work to change them.

While I believe there is very little new in astrology, I find that a chart calculated for the time we first meet somebody reveals the entire nature of the relationship.

Most people who contact me for a consultation have a particular issue in mind, and need to see a clear picture of what may transpire in the future. This often involves a job, a relationship issue, or a new boyfriend or girlfriend the client is curious about.

The traditional way of looking at the relationship between two people is through synastry, or a comparison of the planetary positions of one chart to another. But another more powerful and far more effective divination tool is a type of event chart known as the First Meeting Chart. The First Meeting Chart is simply a chart cast for the moment we first meet someone. Within the framework of that chart all of the potential and/or destiny of that relationship will be shown. It is my experience that this is even more clearly shown than the aspects between the two natal charts themselves.

A First Meeting Chart can be between two people in a business relationship or a love affair, even a friendship. Pay particular attention to the angles of the chart to see if the relationship will be a significant one.

A good example which I can give here is that of the first meeting between myself and the person who took on the job of overhauling my website. In the chart Jupiter was conjunct with the seventh house cusp, indicating a very positive and rewarding business relationship wherein both people would benefit. Mercury of communication was exactly conjunct with the Midheaven indicating a very powerful tenth house relationship.

Pay particular attention to the Nodes in the First Meeting Chart. The nodes often indicate "fated" or karmic relationships. In particular, the north nodes seem to be tied up with "unions" and "coming together", where the south node is more concerned with separation or coming apart. I believe the first meeting chart is an overlooked resource in predictive work. Even if I did not have the birth charts of two people in a relationship, I would be able to determine the whole nature of that relationship by casting a chart for the time they met.

Another branch of astrology which is seldom discussed is horary astrology. Horary astrology gives you a definite answer to a question. It is set up for the time in which an astrologer attempts to answer a question by constructing a horoscope for the exact time at which the question was received and understood by the astrologer.

The answer to the horary question might be a simple yes or no, but is generally more complex with insights into, for example, the motives of the questioner, the motives of others involved in the matter, and the options available to them. Such a question might be, "Will I find my lost cat?" Horary astrology has its own strict system. The position of and aspects to the moon are of prime importance. The person asking the question, or querent, is represented by the ruler of the sign the first house cusp falls on in the horoscope. Planetary aspects to the house cusps are considered more important than in other branches of astrology (although it is the planetary rulers of the houses in question that take precedent in analysis). Other key elements used in horary astrology include the lunar nodes, the planetary antiscia, the fixed stars and the Arabic parts.

Typically, a horary chart is read by first assigning the thing asked about, the quesited, to a particular house in the chart. For instance, asking, "Where is my lost dog?" would be represented by the sixth house, as it is the house that governs small animals (traditionally, smaller than a goat). The house cusp of the sixth house will be in a particular sign, for example Libra. Libra is ruled by Venus, so Venus is considered the significator of the lost dog. Venus's state in the horoscope (its dignity, aspects, etc.) will give clues to the animal's location.

Houses play a more crucial role in horary astrology than they do in other branches of astrology. Any house system preferred by the astrologer may be used, but commonly horary astrologers choose to divide the chart using the Regiomontanus house system.

Understanding the correct house for the context of the question is pivotal to the correct interpretation of a horary question. Everything can be assigned to a house and it is to that house, and its ruler, that the assignation of the quesited is derived. Whatever planet is ruling the sign on the cusp of the house is called the quesited. The context of the horary will often determine the house. For example, if the horary is about matters pertaining to career, the ruler of the 10th House, natural house for careers and jobs, will be the quesited.

A short, non-exhaustive, list of possible associations with houses follows:

The First House

The querent (person asking the question). The querent's physical appearance (hair color and body type for example) or temperament.

The Second House

The querent's finance, wealth and general material and financial possessions. Moveable possessions as opposed to immovable possessions. Allies or supports for the querent, such as your lawyer in court cases. Any personal (moveable) goods and belongings, immovable possessions such as houses are fourth house. Questions about the value of any of your possessions would be second house, for example the buying and selling of a car would be second house (not third).

The Third House

Siblings and neighbours. Any general concern about relatives may be considered third house. Communications and contracts. General comings and goings and short journeys and travels. Letters, e-mails and paperwork. (Cars may be second or third depending on the context of the question – in matters of travel, the third may be used, in matters pertaining to the value of the car, or of buying or selling a car, then the second may be used.)

The Fourth House

Parents. Immovable possessions as opposed to moveable possessions, e.g., your houses, garden, orchard. Mines, oil, buried treasure and anything which comes from the 'bowels of the earth'.

The Fifth House

Children, love affairs, Romance and Sex(as in making love). Gambling, speculation, arguments, games and pleasure. Any venue that caters to our pleasures or provides entertainment including restaurants, clubs, bars and music venues, basically any place you go and have fun.

The Sixth House

Illness and disease or sickness. Also servants, or anyone who works for you, such as a plumber, electrician or anyone in your employ. Pets and small animals, traditionally considered smaller than a goat (larger animals are twelfth house). Work and work environment.

The Seventh House
Marriage, partners and partnerships – both business and personal. Competitors and opponents of all kinds. It is the house of open enemies, by which it is meant enemies that you are aware of. Hidden enemies are the twelfth house. If no other house suffices, use the seventh house to represent 'any old person'.

The Eighth House
Death, fears, anxiety. Sex(in a lustful sense). It is also commonly used as "the house of other people's money". (See 'Turning the chart' below.)

The Ninth House
Long-distance travel, or, travel to unknown or 'exotic' locations. Foreigners and foreign lands. Universities and students of any subject of higher education such as doctors, lawyers, priests and astrologers. Visions, dreams and religion, as well as churches and philosophies. Books. Pilgrimages or journeys for spiritual or religious reasons.

The Tenth House
Career and persons of authority. Heads of state, the government generally, judges and royalty. It is also commonly used to indicate the property belonging to the partner or opponent (see 'Turning the chart' below).

The Eleventh House
Friendships or groups. Wishes, hopes and aspirations. It is considered the house of 'Good Fortune'. Most people know this

as the house of friends and acquaintances. (See 'Turning the chart' below.)

The Twelfth House

Secrets, hidden motives and enemies, captivity, imprisonment and self-undoing. Things not yet known to the querent. Any form of non-voluntary bondage or captivity, monasteries, being voluntary and religious are ninth house. Witchcraft or any manner of secretly undermining the querent.

I have used horary astrology many times when a simple yes or no answer is more important than a long, boring, detailed reading.

How does astrology work? Frankly, I don't know. Many theories exist to explain how astrology works, but none has been proven.

While gravity or electromagnetism are forces by which astrology might possibly function, current scientific wisdom deems these unlikely explanations, though no detailed studies conclusively disprove their involvement.

Quantum physics, a vast scientific frontier, suggests that objects can and do influence other objects that are far away, through forces not currently fully understood by experts, which could hold the missing key to astrological mechanics. While such relatively new ideas challenge long-standing scientific law, they haven't yet been fully explored as a system that verifies the truth of astrology.

Astrology is also seen as an illustration of what psychiatrist Carl Jung called synchronicity, the idea that meaningful coincidences occur between psychological states (i.e., our lives) and outer events, outside any causal relationship. In other words, both planets and people have cycles, which mirror each other through the collectively symbolic language of archetypes (e.g., 'as above, so below'), but do not necessarily cause each other. Of course, synchronicity requires belief in interconnectedness, the intrinsic unity of everything, a rather mystical concept, one perhaps unprovable but not necessarily at odds with modern physics.

After all, astrology does work. Thousands of years of reliable (and often uncanny) results are proof enough for many. But a leap of faith is undeniably required, and we all must decide for ourselves what we believe. I am still working as an astrologer in the year 2016.

Chapter Six

On Board the Flying Saucers

At least five times in my life, I have had some kind of contact with creatures I can only describe as from another world. Most of these contacts have been brief, indirect, or even accidental. At least one, however, was face-to-face.
Alex Tanous

The evidence is overwhelming that Planet Earth is being visited by intelligently controlled extraterrestrial spacecraft. In other words, SOME UFOs are alien spacecraft. Most are not. It's clear from the Opinion Polls and my own experience, that indeed most people accept the notion that SOME UFOs are alien spacecraft. The greater the education, the MORE likely to accept this proposition.
Stanton Friedman

We began to hear worldwide rumours of Unidentified Flying Objects as early as 1945. These rumours are founded either upon visions or upon actual phenomena. The usual story about the UFOs is that they are some kind of spacecraft coming from other planets or even from the fourth dimension.
Carl Jung, *Memories, Dreams, Reflections*

I was sitting in the studios of Talk Radio Station WBT in Charlotte, North Carolina. With me was my co-host Gene Grant. Together we were presenting a three-hour talk show from nine to midnight. My first guest was physicist and UFO researcher Stanton Friedman. Stan is known as the "grandfather of UFO studies". He asserted to me on that show that lies by the U.S. government about a crashed flying saucer in New Mexico in July 1947 have gone on for over sixty years. He is the original civilian investigator on the Roswell UFO crash.

Nuclear Physicist-Lecturer Stanton T. Friedman received his BSc. and MSc. degrees in physics from the University of Chicago in 1955 and 1956. He was employed for 14 years as a nuclear physicist by such companies as GE, GM, Westinghouse, TRW Systems, Aerojet General Nucleonics, and McDonnell Douglas working in such highly advanced, classified, eventually cancelled programmes as nuclear aircraft, fission and fusion rockets, and various compact nuclear power plants for space and terrestrial applications.

He became interested in UFOs in 1958, and since 1967 has lectured about them at more than 600 colleges and 100 professional groups in 50 U.S. states, 10 Canadian provinces and 18 other countries in addition to various nuclear consulting efforts. He has published more than 90 UFO papers and has appeared on hundreds of radio and TV programmes including on Larry King in 2007 and twice in 2008, and many documentaries. He is the original civilian investigator of the Roswell Incident and co-authored *Crash at Corona: The Definitive Study of the Roswell Incident*. *TOP SECRET/MAJIC*, his controversial book about the Majestic 12 group, established in 1947 to deal with alien technology, was published in 1996 and went through 6 printings. An expanded new edition was published in 2005. Stan was presented with a Lifetime UFO Achievement Award in Leeds, England, in 2002, by UFO Magazine of the UK. He is co-author with Kathleen Marden (Betty Hill's niece) of a book in 2007: *Captured! The Betty and Barney Hill UFO Experience*. The City of Fredericton, New Brunswick, declared August 27, 2007, Stanton Friedman Day. His book *Flying Saucers and Science* was published in June 2008 and is in its third printing. His newest book, also co-authored with Kathleen Marden, is *Science Was Wrong* released in June 2010.

He has provided written testimony to Congressional Hearings, appeared twice at the UN, and been a pioneer in many aspects of ufology including Roswell, Majestic 12, The Betty Hill-Marjorie Fish star map work, analysis of the Delphos, Kansas, physical trace case, crashed saucers, flying saucer technology, and challenges to the S.E.T.I. (Silly Effort to Investigate) cultists. He has spoken at more MUFON Symposia than anyone else.

I found my interview with him absorbing and enlightening. "Most unidentified flying objects are not alien spacecraft. I'm not interested in those. Most isotopes aren't fissionable. I'm not interested in those either."

In 1968 Stan told a committee of the U.S. House of Representatives that the evidence suggests that Earth is being visited by intelligently controlled extraterrestrial vehicles. Stan also stated he believed that UFO sightings were consistent with magnetohydrodynamic propulsion.

In 1996, after researching and fact checking the Majestic 12 documents, Stan said that there was no substantive grounds for dismissing their authenticity.

In 2004, on George Noory's Coast to Coast radio show, Stan debated Seth Shostak, the SETI Institute's Senior Astronomer. Like Stan, Shostak also believes in the existence of intelligent life other than humans; however, unlike Stan, he doesn't believe such life is now on Earth or is related to UFO sightings.

Stan has hypothesized that UFOs may originate from relatively nearby sun-like stars.

A piece of evidence that he often cites with respect to this hypothesis is the 1964 star map drawn by alleged alien abductee Betty Hill during a hypnosis session, which she said was shown to her during her abduction. Astronomer Marjorie Fish constructed a three-dimensional map of nearby sun-like stars and claimed a good match from the perspective of Zeta Reticuli, about 39 light years distant. The fit of the Hill/Fish star maps was hotly debated in the December 1974 edition of Astronomy Magazine, with Stan and others defending the statistical validity of the match.

During my three-hour interview with Stan on WBT, I had a variety of callers, some supportive of Stan's view, some not. One of my more interesting calls came from a man in New York:

Well, the government claims that they were covering up Project Mogel, that's why when they said it was a UFO that landed, they had to quickly cover it up. They came out and said, "You can't say it was a UFO, now we've got to go back to a weather balloon." Also, with the bodies, they said it was doing experiments with chimps.

Stan's reply was about the best I had ever heard:

You know, it was crazy about Roswell. There were four different explanations. First, a press release said a crashed flying saucer was recovered. Then it was oh no, sorry, it was a radar reflector, weather balloon combination. Then, fast forward forty some years, it was a super-secret mogul. Mogul consisted of twenty to twenty-five balloons, just standard. Remember the old-fashioned weather balloons that you could buy at the surplus stores? Twenty-five of them at twenty-foot intervals and sono bouys and ballast tanks and stuff like that. There's no way that the guys at the 509th couldn't identify a weather balloon. And the wreckage, the stuff it was made out of, could be torn by a three year old, which was not true of what was found at Roswell. Then they came up with the crash test dummies. That's my favourite. None were dropped ... I mean they were dropping lots of them, but not until after 1953. Roswell was 1947, so they invented time-travel for crash test dummies.

During our interview I found that Stan's forty years of UFO investigation has uncovered some remarkable things. Some of the witnesses to the Roswell incident are still living today and

Stan has interviewed most of them. In the summer of 2011, I started digging around to find one of them myself. He was Jesse Marcel, Jr., now deceased, the son of Major Jesse Marcel who was sent to recover the debris of the crash. I spoke to him by telephone and this is what he told me:

My dad was the base intelligence officer at the Roswell Army Air Field in 1947. Something crashed on the Foster Ranch which was about seventy-five miles north of Roswell. The rancher didn't know what it was, the sheriff didn't know what it was, so they contacted Col. Blanchard who was the base commander at the Roswell Army Air Field, and he sent my dad out to investigate what this was. The rancher took him out to a debris field where debris was scattered all over the place. What they did was to gather up pieces of this and drive it back into Roswell. As it happens, our house was on the way to the air base. He came home one night with several boxes of debris that he had packed into the car. I was eleven years old at the time. I started looking at the foil. He took a sledge hammer and whacked it and it couldn't be dented. The next thing I looked at were some little beams that were lying on the floor. When I first saw it I noticed there some kind of writing on the inside surface of these, which looked like Egyptian hieroglyphics. They were like geometric symbols, and if you held them up to the light, they would reflect back at you. Years later, when I was in Washington, I was contacted by a man who asked me to meet him in the Capitol building. I met with this man who told me that just about everything I already knew about the Roswell crash was true and that he was then trying to find out for himself who had the debris now. I asked him when he thought that the truth would finally be revealed to people about what really happened. His reply was, "If it were up to me it would be yesterday, but it is not up to me."

For the unenlightened, there were several reports of alien bodies that were recovered. Glenn Dennis, a young mortician who worked for Ballard Funeral Homes, was asked about the availability of small hermetically sealed caskets and for his recommendations on the preservation of bodies that had been exposed to the elements for several days. Glenn Dennis kept drawings of aliens that a nurse had sketched on a napkin during their meeting.

The Ballard Funeral Home in Roswell had a contract to provide ambulance and mortuary services for Roswell Army Air Field. Glenn Dennis, a young Mortician who worked for Ballard Funeral Homes, received several phone calls from the Mortuary Officer at the air field prior to learning of the recovery of the wreckage. Glenn Dennis was asked about the availability of small hermetically sealed caskets and for his recommendations on the preservation of bodies that had been exposed to the elements for several days. His curiosity aroused, Glenn Dennis visited the Base Hospital that evening and was forcibly escorted from the building. This behaviour only incited Glenn Dennis' curiosity and he arranged to meet a nurse from the Base Hospital on the following day in a coffee house. The nurse had been in attendance during autopsies performed on "... several small non-human bodies ...". Glenn Dennis kept drawings of aliens that the nurse had sketched on a napkin during their meeting. This meeting was to be their last and Glenn Dennis could learn no more about the alien bodies, as the nurse was abruptly transferred to England within the next few days.

There is wide speculation about where the bodies were taken after they left Roswell. Tales of crashed UFO parts and alien bodies have been told about Wright-Patterson Air Force Base since the 1947 Roswell incident and now include a secondhand report filed today as Case 58327 from the Mutual UFO Network (MUFON) witness reporting database.

The report was filed by the grandchild of the woman who

received the information firsthand in about 1960 who explains that his grandparents lived in Dayton, Ohio, for many years prior to 1964:

> A close friend retired from Wright Patterson Air Force Base. He was high ranking. My grandmother, who was the most witty, honest and candid person I've ever met asked him if it were true about the alien craft and possibly the alien bodies being stored at the base.

The witness stated that he will never forget how the man responded as told to him by his grandmother: "He said, 'If the public knew what was at the base from the Roswell incident, there would be a general panic amongst the public.'"

Senator Barry Goldwater suspected the bodies were at Wright Patterson. In 1994, in an interview conducted by Larry King and broadcast on CNN, Goldwater said:

> I think at Wright-Patterson, if you could get into certain places, you'd find out what the Air Force and the government does know about UFOs. Reportedly, a spaceship landed. It was all hushed up. I called Curtis LeMay and I said, 'General, I know we have a room at Wright-Patterson where you put all this secret stuff. Could I go in there?' I've never heard General LeMay get mad, but he got madder than hell at me, cussed me out, and said, 'Don't ever ask me that question again!'

On July 9th the Roswell Daily Record revealed that the wreckage had been found on the J.B. Foster Ranch. Mac Brazel was so harassed that he became sorry he had ever reported his find to the Chaves County Sheriff.

In the following days virtually every witness to the crash wreckage and the subsequent recovery efforts was either abruptly transferred or seemed to disappear from the face of the earth. This led to suspicions that an extraordinary event was the subject of a deliberate government cover-up. Over the years, books, interviews and articles from a number of military personnel, who had been involved with the incident, have added to the suspicions of a deliberate cover-up.

Flight engineer Robert Porter signed a sworn affidavit about his part in the cover-up.

(1) My name is Robert R. Porter

(2) My address is: XXXXXXXXXX

(3) I am (X) retired ( ) employed as: _____

(4) In July 1947, I was a Master Sergeant in the U.S. Army Air Force, stationed at Roswell, New Mexico. I was a flight engineer. My job entailed taking care of the engines in flight, maintaining weight and balance, and I was responsible for fuel management. We mostly flew B-29s.

(5) On this occasion, I was a member of the crew which flew parts of what we were told was a flying saucer to Fort Worth. The people on board included: Lt. Col. Payne Jennings, the Deputy Commander of the base; Lt. Col. Robert I. Barrowclough; Maj. Herb Wunderlich; and Maj. Jesse Marcel. Capt. William E. Anderson said it was from a flying saucer. After we arrived, the material was transferred to a B-25. I was told they were going to Wright Field in Dayton, Ohio.

(6) I was involved in loading the B-29 with the material, which was wrapped in packages with wrapping paper. One of the pieces was triangle-shaped, about 2 1/2 feet across the bottom. The rest were in small packages, about the size of a shoe box. The brown paper was held with tape.

(7) The material was extremely lightweight. When I picked it up, it was just like picking up an empty package. We loaded the triangle-shaped package and three shoe box-sized packages into the plane. All of the packages could have fit into the trunk of a car.

(8) After we landed at Fort Worth, Col Jennings told us to

take care of maintenance of the plane and that after a guard was posted, we could eat lunch. When we came back from lunch, they told us they had transferred the material to a B-25. They told us the material was a weather balloon, but I'm certain it wasn't a weather balloon. I think the government should let the people know what's going on.

(9) I have not been paid or given anything of value to make this statement, which is the truth to the best of my recollection.

Signed: Robert R. Porter

June 7, 1991

Signature witnessed by:

Ruth N. Ford 6/7/91

In 1979 Jesse Marcel was interviewed regarding his role in the recovery of the wreckage. Jesse Marcel stated, "... it would not burn ... that stuff weighs nothing, it's so thin, it isn't any thicker than the tinfoil in a pack of cigarettes. It wouldn't bend. We even tried making a dent in it with a 16-pound sledge hammer. And there was still no dent in it." Officers who had been stationed at Wright Field in Dayton, Ohio (where the wreckage was taken) at the time of the incident have supported Jesse Marcel's claims. Nobody knows for sure. There have been reports that the bodies as well as the wreckage is in Florida, not in Ohio at all. One of these reports came from the late Jackie Gleason.

The fine actor and comedian Jackie Gleason will forever be associated with his role of bus driver Ralph Cramden on the popular TV series, "The Honeymooners". But there was another side to Jackie that few people know about. Gleason was an extremely serious armchair UFO researcher, and prided himself on his huge collection of UFO-related books, which numbered into the thousands. As soon as a new title came out, even in Europe or the UK, Jackie had a copy. Little did he suspect that his interest in that topic would one day gain him access to something that most people would never even believe, and would leave others who shared his interests either sceptical or forever jealous.

It was a chance conversation one afternoon, back in 1974 in Florida, while Jackie was playing golf with one of his regular partners, President Richard Nixon. Jackie had mentioned his interest in UFOs and his large collection of books, and the president admitted that he also shared Jackie's interest and had a sizeable collection of UFO-oriented materials of his own. At the time, the president said little about what he actually knew, but things were to change drastically later on that same night.

One can only imagine Gleason's surprise when President Nixon showed up at his house around midnight, completely alone and driving his own private car. When Jackie asked him why he was there, Nixon told him that he wanted to take him somewhere and show him something. He got into the president's car, and they ended up at the gates of Homestead Air Force Base. They passed through security and drove to the far end of the base, to a tightly-guarded building. At this point, I will quote directly from Gleason himself, from an interview he gave to UFO researcher and author Larry Warren:

> We drove to the very far end of the base in a segregated area, finally stopping near a well-guarded building. The security police saw us coming and just sort of moved back as we passed them and entered the structure. There were a number of labs we passed through first before we entered a section where Nixon pointed out what he said was the wreckage from a flying saucer, enclosed in several large cases. Next, we went into an inner chamber and there were six or eight of what looked like glass-topped Coke freezers. Inside them were the mangled remains of what I took to be children. Then – upon closer examination – I saw that some of the other figures looked quite old. Most of them were terribly mangled as if they had been in an accident.

Gleason was understandably excited by all of this, but also quite traumatized, and said he couldn't eat or sleep properly for weeks afterwards, and found himself drinking heavily until he was able to regain his composure. His wife at the time, Beverly, recalls him being out very late that night and speaking excitedly about what he had seen when he returned home. Later on, however, when she and Gleason were splitting up and she told the story to a writer at Esquire Magazine, which printed it in an article, relations between her and the entertainer deteriorated and Gleason became very upset and angry that the story had been made public. For this reason many people, including Beverly herself, have wondered at the truth of the story. However, in his interview with Larry Warren, who was invited to Jackie's house in person because Gleason wanted to hear firsthand about Warren's experience at Bentwaters Air Force Base in England, it was clear that Jackie was being honest and sincere:

> You could tell that he was very sincere – he took the whole affair very seriously, and I could tell that he wanted to get the matter off his chest, and that was why he was telling me all of this. Jackie felt just like I do, that the government needs to 'come clean,' and tell us all it knows about space visitors. It's time they stopped lying to the public and release all the evidence they have. When they do, then we'll all be able to see the same things the late Jackie Gleason did.

The United States government's knowledge about UFOs and their occupants exists at the very highest levels of security, above even atomic weapons and things of that nature. Information is imparted on a strictly "need to know" basis, and this has left even many presidents in the dark on the subject. Obviously, Richard Nixon wasn't one of them. One can only imagine what technology and evidence of life outside of this Earth exists in the back corners and hidden labs of the American military, but for anyone who doesn't believe that this situation is real, this story about Jackie Gleason is just the very tiny tip of the iceberg.

In the summer of 1989, while on a visit to Maine, my friend Alex Tanous told me the following story about his encounter with aliens from another world:

"It happened when a friend told me of some strange people, who'd been seen in New Mexico near a major experimental government installation," Alex told me.

My mind immediately flashed back to the 1960s television show, "The Invaders" in which David Vincent encounters aliens, seemingly always near an abandoned power station or similar installation. "It began one lost night on a lonely country road seeking a short-cut that he never found. It began with a closed, deserted diner, and a man too long without sleep to continue his journey," went the opening to the show.

But this was no TV show. Alex continued, "These people – three men – had been seen on many occasions near this installation. Local residents said the men had been there for years – ever since the first experimental atomic explosion at Alamogordo in 1945.

"What's strange about the men?" Alex asked.

"Well," said my friend, "they just don't look quite right. You can't put your finger on it. It's more like they're imitation human beings."

"Don't you have anything more specific?"

"Most people think there's something wrong with their eyes, I don't know anything more than that."

"At any rate," Alex told me, "arrangements were made for me to fly to New Mexico and try to make contact with one of these individuals. The parties who made these arrangements wanted to have my psychic impressions of these people, if that's what they were.

"And so I flew to New Mexico. The plan was for me to frequent a diner at which the men had often been seen. The confrontation came almost immediately. I walked into the diner, along with a man who'd seen the people in question and could identify them. He scanned the room, then drew me aside.

"That's one of them," he said, pointing as discreetly as possible.

"I followed the gesture. My informant had singled out a man sitting at the end of the counter.

"All right," I said, "I'll take it from here."

"I took a seat at the counter a few empty stools away from the man who'd been pointed out to me," Alex told me, "and tried to think of a way to approach him, to engage him in conversation so I could get some impression of him.

"Finally, I looked his way, about to ask him to pass the sugar. Our eyes met. A tremendous vibration went through me. For a few seconds our eyes held. I'd never seen any eyes like his before or since. They were like Bette Davis's eyes – only in reverse. Where hers pop out, his popped in, if you can imagine that. During our eye contact, I heard him speak to me in my mind.

"Why have you come here? Why do you do this? You are just like one of us."

"As I heard those words, all desire to speak to him left me. I got up from my seat and left the diner – to the intense disappointment of those who'd arranged the trip. But I could do nothing else.

"I don't know if this man was from another planet. I don't know who he was or what he was. All I know is that I felt a bizarre energy, and that I got a message from him. It was one of the strangest experiences in my life. Since then, I understand none of the three men have been seen in the area again."

For as long as I knew him Alex had this unusual ability to pick up and sense things about people just by seeing them or shaking hands with them. When he was on the TV show, "To Tell the Truth", he met abductee Charles Hickson, also a guest on the show.

"When I shook hands with him," Alex said, "I felt this same energy pass through me. There was something different about the man, as if he had been changed by his experience."

On the evening of October 11, 1973, co-workers 42-year-old Charles Hickson and 19-year-old Calvin Parker told the Jackson County, Mississippi Sheriff's office they were fishing off a pier on the west bank of the Pascagoula River in Mississippi when they heard a whirring/whizzing sound, saw two flashing blue lights and an oval shaped object 30-40 feet across and 8-10 feet high. Parker and Hickson claimed that they were "conscious but paralyzed" while three "creatures" took them aboard the object and subjected them to an examination before releasing them.

Within days, Pascagoula was the centre of an international news story, with reporters swarming the town. Ufologists James Harder of the Aerial Phenomena Research Organization and J. Allen Hynek interviewed the two men. Harder attempted to hypnotize them and concluded Hickson and Parker "experienced an extraterrestrial phenomena", while Hynek believed they had "a very real, frightening experience". Hickson later appeared on talk shows, gave lectures and interviews, and in 1983 authored a self-published book *UFO Contact at Pascagoula.* Hickson claimed additional encounters with aliens in 1974, alleging that the aliens told him they were "peaceful". Parker later attended UFO conventions and in 1993 started a company called "UFO Investigations" to produce television stories about UFOs. Charles Hickson died at age 80 on September 9, 2011.

Charles Hickson never regretted the notoriety that came his way after he told authorities he encountered an unidentified flying object and its occupants 40 years ago on the banks of the Pascagoula River. Until his death in 2011, Hickson told his story to anyone who would listen.

But Calvin Parker Jr., the other man present for one of the most high-profile UFO cases in American history, has never come to terms with what he still says was a visit with grey, crab-clawed creatures from somewhere else. He says the encounter on Oct. 11, 1973, turned his life upside down.

"This is something I really didn't want to happen," Parker told The Associated Press as the 40th anniversary of the encounter approached.

While on my radio show on WBT, Stanton Friedman also discussed with me the story of the Betty and Barney Hill alien abduction in New Hampshire. Oddly enough, Alex Tanous was also friends with Betty Hill. Alex used to tell me bits and pieces of the story that were not reported in the press. Stan, together with Kathleen Marden, wrote a book about the Hill abduction, *Captured! The Betty and Barney Hill UFO Experience.* Having read the book myself, I can definitely state that cynics and debunkers have got it wrong when they say that the Hills had read books about UFOs and seen television programmes on the subject before the incident. They had never read any books, nor seen any shows. It has become one of the most famous cases of alien abduction in history.

The Hills lived in Portsmouth, New Hampshire. Barney (1922–1969) was employed by the U.S. Postal Service, while Betty (1919–2004) was a social worker. Active in a Unitarian congregation, the Hills were also members of the NAACP and community leaders, and Barney. According to a variety of reports given by the Hills, the alleged UFO sighting happened on September 19, 1961, around 10:30 p.m. The Hills were driving back to Portsmouth from a vacation in Niagara Falls and Montreal. There were only a few other cars on the road as they made their way home to New Hampshire's seacoast. Just south of Lancaster, New Hampshire, Betty claimed to have observed a bright point of light in the sky that moved from below the moon and the planet Jupiter, upward to the west of the moon. While Barney navigated U.S. Route 3, Betty reasoned that she was observing a falling star, only it moved upward. Since it moved erratically and grew bigger and brighter, Betty urged

Barney to stop the car for a closer look, as well as to walk their dog, Delsey. Barney stopped at a scenic picnic area just south of Twin Mountain. Worried about the presence of bears, Barney retrieved a pistol that he kept in the trunk of the car.

Betty, through binoculars, observed an "odd-shaped" craft flashing multi-coloured lights travel across the face of the moon. Because her sister had confided to her about having a flying saucer sighting several years earlier, Betty thought it might be what she was observing. Through binoculars Barney observed what he reasoned was a commercial airliner travelling toward Vermont on its way to Montreal. However, he soon changed his mind, because without looking as if it had turned, the craft rapidly descended in his direction. This observation caused Barney to realize "this object that was a plane was not a plane". He quickly returned to the car and drove toward Franconia Notch, a narrow, mountainous stretch of the road.

The Hills claimed that they continued driving on the isolated road, moving very slowly through Franconia Notch in order to observe the object as it came even closer. At one point, the object passed above a restaurant and signal tower on top of Cannon Mountain. It passed over the mountain and came out near the Old Man of the Mountain. Betty testified that it was at least one and a half times the length of the granite cliff profile, which was 40 feet (12 m) long, and that seemed to be rotating. The couple watched as the silent, illuminated craft moved erratically and bounced back and forth in the night sky. As they drove along Route 3 through Franconia Notch, they stated that it seemed to be playing a game of cat and mouse with them.

Approximately one mile south of Indian Head, they said, the object rapidly descended toward their vehicle causing Barney to stop directly in the middle of the highway. The huge, silent craft hovered approximately 80–100 feet (24–30 m) above the Hills' 1957 Chevrolet Bel Air and filled the entire field of the windshield. It reminded Barney of a huge pancake. Carrying his pistol in his pocket, he stepped away from the vehicle and moved closer to the object. Using the binoculars, Barney claimed to have seen about 8 to 11 humanoid figures who were peering out of the craft's windows, seeming to look at him. In unison, all but one figure moved to what appeared to be a panel on the rear wall of the hallway that encircled the front portion of the craft. The one remaining figure continued to look at Barney and communicated a message telling him to "stay where you are and keep looking". Barney had a conscious, continuous recollection of observing the humanoid forms wearing glossy black uniforms and black caps. Red lights on what appeared to be bat-wing fins began to telescope out of the sides of the craft and a long structure descended from the bottom of the craft. The silent craft approached to what Barney estimated was within 50–80 feet overhead and 300 feet away from him. On October 21, 1961, Barney reported to NICAP Investigator Walter Webb, that the "beings were somehow not human".

Barney "tore" the binoculars away from his eyes and ran back to his car. In a near hysterical state, he told Betty, "They're going to capture us!" He saw the object again shift its location to directly above the vehicle. He drove away at high speed, telling Betty to look for the object. She rolled down the window and looked up, but saw only darkness above them, even though it was a bright, starry night.

Almost immediately, the Hills heard a rhythmic series of beeping or buzzing sounds which they said seemed to bounce off the trunk of their vehicle. The car vibrated and a tingling sensation passed through the Hills' bodies. Betty touched the metal on the passenger door expecting to feel an electric shock, but felt only the vibration. The Hills said that at this point in time they experienced the onset of an altered state of consciousness that left their minds dulled. A second series of code-like beeping or buzzing sounds returned the couple to full consciousness. They found that they had travelled nearly 35 miles (56 km) south but had only vague, spotty memories of this section of road. They recalled making a sudden unplanned turn, encountering a roadblock, and observing a fiery orb in the road.

On September 21, Betty telephoned Pease Air Force Base to report their UFO encounter, though for fear of being labelled eccentric, she withheld some of the details. On September 22, Major Paul W. Henderson telephoned the Hills for a more detailed interview. Henderson's report, dated September 26, determined that the Hills had probably misidentified the planet Jupiter. (This was later changed to "optical condition", "inversion" and "insufficient data".) (Report 100-1-61, Air Intelligence Information Record.) His report was forwarded to Project Blue Book, the U.S. Air Force's UFO research project.

Within days of the encounter, Betty borrowed a UFO book from a local library. It had been written by retired Marine Corps Major Donald E. Keyhoe, who was also the head of NICAP, a civilian UFO research group. On September 26, Betty wrote to Keyhoe. She related the full story, including the details about the humanoid figures that Barney had observed through binoculars. Betty wrote that she and Barney were considering hypnosis to help recall what had happened. Her letter was eventually passed on to Walter N. Webb, a Boston astronomer and NICAP member.

Webb met with the Hills on October 21, 1961. In a six-hour interview, the Hills related all they could remember of the UFO encounter. Barney asserted that he had developed a sort of "mental block" and that he suspected there were some portions of the event that he did not wish to remember. He described in detail all that he could remember about the craft and the appearance of the "somehow not human" figures aboard the craft. Webb stated that "they were telling the truth and the incident probably occurred exactly as reported except for some minor uncertainties and technicalities that must be tolerated in any such observations where human judgment is involved (e.g., exact time and length of visibility, apparent sizes of object and occupants, distance and height of object, etc.)".

In December 1962 the Hills were referred to Dr Benjamin Simon, a Boston psychiatrist. Simon figured prominently in John Fuller's book, *Interrupted Journey*. Through repeated hypnosis sessions Simon came to believe that the Hills believed the story they were telling. He could not, however, bring himself to believe they were abducted by aliens and said as much in Fuller's book. Simon was not going to risk his reputation as a psychiatrist.

Simon hypnotized Barney first. His recall of witnessing non-human figures was quite emotional, punctuated with expressions of fear, emotional outbursts and incredulity. Barney said that, due to his fear, he kept his eyes closed for much of the abduction and physical examination. Based on these early responses, Simon told Barney that he would not remember the hypnosis sessions until he was certain he could remember them without being further traumatized.

Under hypnosis (as was consistent with his conscious recall), Barney reported that the binocular strap had broken when he ran from the UFO back to his car. He recalled driving the car away from the UFO, but that afterwards he felt irresistibly compelled to pull off the road, and drive into the woods. He eventually sighted six men standing in the dirt road. The car stalled and three of the men approached the car. They told Barney to not fear them. He was still anxious, however, and he reported that the leader told Barney to close his eyes. While hypnotized, Barney said, "I felt like the eyes had pushed into my eyes."

Barney described the beings as generally similar to Betty's hypnotic, not dream, recollection. The beings often stared into his eyes, said Barney, with a terrifying, mesmerizing effect. Under hypnosis, Barney said things like, "Oh, those eyes. They're there in my brain," (from his first hypnosis session) and "I was told to close my eyes because I saw two eyes coming close to mine, and I felt like the eyes had pushed into my eyes," (from his second hypnosis session) and "All I see are these eyes ... I'm not even afraid that they're not connected to a body. They're just there. They're just up close to me, pressing against my eyes."

Barney related that he and Betty were taken onto the disc-shaped craft, where they were separated. He was escorted to a room by three of the men and told to lie on a small rectangular exam table. Unlike Betty, Barney's narrative of the exam was less detailed, as he continued to keep his eyes closed for most of the exam. A cup-like device was placed over his genitals. He did not experience an orgasm though Barney thought that a sperm sample had been taken. The men scraped his skin, and peered in his ears and mouth. A thin tube or cylinder was inserted into his anus and quickly removed. Someone felt his spine, and seemed to be counting his vertebrae.

Under hypnosis, Betty's account was very similar to the events of her five dreams about the UFO abduction, but there were also notable differences. Details pertaining to her capture and release were different. The technology on the craft was different. The short men had a significantly different physical appearance than the ones in her dreams. The sequential order of the abduction event was also different from in Betty's dream account. She filled in many details that were not in her dreams and contradicted some of her dream content. Interestingly, Barney's and Betty's memories in hypnotic regression were consistent but contradicted some of the information in Betty's dreams.

Betty exhibited considerable emotional distress during her capture and examination. Simon ended one session early because tears were flowing down her cheeks and she was in considerable agony.

After extensive hypnosis sessions, Simon speculated that Barney's recall of the UFO encounter was possibly a fantasy inspired by Betty's dreams. Though Simon admitted this hypothesis did not explain every aspect of the experience, he thought it was the most plausible and consistent explanation.

Barney rejected this idea, noting that while their memories were in some regards interlocking, there were also portions of both their narratives that were unique to each. Barney was now ready to accept that they had been abducted by the occupants of a UFO, though he never embraced it as fully as Betty did.

Though the Hills and Simon disagreed about the nature of the case, they all concurred that the hypnosis sessions were effective: the Hills were no longer tormented by anxiety about the UFO encounter.

Afterwards, Simon wrote an article about the Hills for the journal *Psychiatric Opinion*, explaining his conclusions that the case was a singular psychological aberration.

In 1966, writer John G. Fuller secured the cooperation of the Hills and Simon and wrote the book *The Interrupted Journey* about the case. The book included a copy of Betty's sketch of the "star map". The book was a quick success, and went through several printings.

In 1968, Marjorie Fish of Oak Harbor, Ohio read Fuller's *The Interrupted Journey*. She was an elementary school teacher and amateur astronomer. Intrigued by the "star map", Fish wondered if it might be "deciphered" to determine which star system the UFO came from. Assuming that one of the fifteen stars on the map must represent the Earth's Sun, Fish constructed a three-dimensional model of nearby Sun-like stars using thread and beads, basing stellar distances on those published in the 1969 *Gliese Star Catalogue*. Studying thousands of vantage points over several years, the only one that seemed to match the Hill map was from the viewpoint of the double star system of Zeta Reticuli.

During our radio interview on WBT, Stanton Friedman told me it was his opinion that the craft in the Hill case was from Zeta Reticuli.

Although I never met Betty Hill, Alex Tanous told me several times that he felt psychically that Betty was relating a genuine experience and not one of imagination.

Since the Hill case, there are literally thousands of people who have reported that they have been abducted and/or been "on board flying saucers". Yet I know of only one person living today who has openly stated he has interacted with aliens with government knowledge. That man is Clifford Stone. I interviewed him by telephone while I was in Colorado Springs in August 2011.

Clifford Stone is unique among those experiencing and investigating UFO and ET phenomena. He spent 22 years in the US Army as a part of an extremely elite and secret group that was rapidly dispatched to crash sites in order to recover UFO or ET craft, bodies, and artefacts. Since his retirement from the Army, he has devoted his time to a diligent Freedom of Information Act search of government archives. He maintains that we have knowledge that intelligent life is visiting this planet in craft capable of travelling distances of many light years very quickly; effectively bypassing acceptably known physics. Further, he stresses that our recovery of these ET craft and artefacts has allowed our government to make staggering scientific gains of great potential benefit to the world. He maintains, as do many others, that this information is held in deeply secret programmes beyond Constitutional controls and safeguards, and that despite the end of the cold war, those controlling these 'black projects' have continued to keep these important discoveries to themselves and for motives known only to them.

Sgt. Stone is coming forward with his story to encourage citizens and our elected officials to open investigations and end this Constitutional bypass by a powerful and covert organization operating under our noses and in our skies.

Clifford Stone was born in Portsmouth, Ohio. At an early age, he has memories of being contacted by ETs and that contact continues today. At age eight, he was befriended by an Air Force captain and that relationship continued through his early adult life. During the Vietnam war, he felt an obligation to enlist in the Air Force but was rejected due to a skin affliction and classified 4F. He was advised by his friend, the captain, to try the Army and after a 'lenient' medical examination, he was allowed into the Army as a clerk typist, a job he never had to fulfil.

Within weeks, he found himself picked up in a staff car on the pretence of seeing a low ranking friend with a job at the Pentagon. On arrival, his friend's clearances allowed them into levels beneath the Pentagon, onto a tram, and soon he found himself thrust into a room and circumstances beyond imagination. His career was never normal, and for a newly minted soldier, he was suddenly thrust into the USA's deepest secrets: ETs are real and we are successfully recovering many of their craft intact as well as hundreds of ET artefacts worldwide. Further, we are familiar with much of their technologies and have in fact, back engineered some of the ET gear. After22 years of being on the scene with ET craft and dead, wounded, and living ETs, Sgt. Stone is highly qualified as an expert in ET tech, black ops organizations/procedures, and the potentiality of ET contact to mankind.

Stone maintains that this secrecy is unconstitutional and beyond control and knowledge of our elected officials. Thereby, this represents a government hidden within our society with tremendous assets, funding, and knowledge.

Further, he feels this secrecy has split large parts of the citizenry into those that have seen UFO or ET craft/beings and those that place these observers in a category as something less than competent. Much of the malaise and mistrust of government can be attributed to a remarkable majority of its citizenry seeing or believing in these objects while the government and its officials and representatives deny or lack the courage to disclose what is now obvious. Also, the considerable scientific skills and assets of the world are for the most part, diverted by this bias from working on projects generations ahead of current understanding. This continues to allow important discoveries and advances within the control of the few.

Stone is bravely, and with resistance from covert quarters, coming forward with his story to do the following: He urges those in the know to admit that UFOs seen by millions worldwide are both ET and our own 'back engineered' ET-style craft; release the abundant information and materials that show intelligent life is visiting our planet and has been monitored by numerous governments for decades; provide the information that will allow our Constitutional government to take back control of these deeply compartmented programmes and restore confidence and trust in our system of government and military organizations. And at last, urge our government to finally entrust its citizens and the world with the truth about ET existence and technologies.

There exists a universal curiosity, increasing over time, about the UFO mystery. I have seen it grow, and have observed an improvement in media coverage about UFOs over the years. The more we learn, the more confounding it becomes. Still, many people continue to think the subject is based on fantasy or mistaken identity, or some kind of joke and therefore a waste of time. My hope is that these people do some research on their own and then draw a conclusion. Mainstream scientists have been too afraid to risk their reputations. A good example of this is the late scientist and astronomer Carl Sagan who was a classmate of Stanton Friedman's at the University of Chicago. Stan told me during a talk radio interview on WBT, Charlotte, North Carolina that Sagan worked on a number of top secret government projects to do with space and was privy to inside information. In Stan's words, "He was constantly talking about the possibility of extraterrestrial life but blew every opportunity to announce to the world that the aliens are already here."

A good example of how far a scientist will go to misrepresent the facts in order to save his reputation is illustrated in Stan's ad in Kathleen Marden's book, *Science Was Wrong*, in which Sagan deliberately misrepresented the facts about the Betty and Barney Hill abduction case:

> It is difficult to understand why a prominent astronomer such as Sagan would deliberately misrepresent the Hill UFO encounter to more than 400 million viewers, yet the dramatization of his "Cosmos" television series depicts a nervous Betty gazing upward through torrential downpours with windshield wipers swishing, while at the same time she turns the knob on the radio to eliminate static. The truth is that the radio was off and the weather was clear.

Why the deception? Simply, because as Charles Fort put it, any announcement about the "damned facts" being true would be too radical a departure from the accepted ideas of mainstream science and put that scientist's reputation at risk. Until scientists take that risk, nothing will change.

Chapter Seven

You Must Be Dreaming

And if we happen to have a precognitive dream, how can we possibly ascribe it to our own powers? After all, often we do not even know, until sometime afterward, that the dream represented foreknowledge, or knowledge of something that happened at a distance.
Carl Jung, *Memories, Dreams, Reflections*

Ever since I was in my early twenties, I have dreamed of things that occurred later. The first of these experiences took place when I was about twenty-one. I had a strange dream, which repeated itself several times during the night. I heard a voice say: Gallant Boy will win you a lot of money". Next day I told a friend, Steve Griffin, about it. He laughed and said, "Gallant Boy is a race horse and is running on Saturday," which was a few days off. Out of curiosity I asked him to back it for me as I had no knowledge of racing or betting. Well, it won, and if I remember rightly, at ten to one. It won many times after that, and if I had backed it each time, I would have made a lot of money. The same year I dreamt of Golden Lad, which won at twenty to one, and of many others.

Precognitive dreams, or dreams that predict a future event are not uncommon. There is obviously some principle operating in the universe which allows us to have a sneak preview of what lies ahead.

I will discuss the prediction of future events made by psychics, mediums and clairvoyants in another chapter, but here I want to discuss the precognitive dream. It is one that baffles me even more than a prediction made by a medium.

My friend the late Alex Tanous had many such dreams in his

youth, including those that warned of disaster. In one dream he dreamt that he was invited by a friend to go for a car drive. Without thinking he said (in the dream), "I cannot go today." In the dream his lips spoke without his consent. The next day an accident occurred. His friend went for his drive with his son. They stopped to have lunch. While they were returning to the car, another car struck the boy and killed him.

There are those who've claimed to have dreams or premonitions regarding a major airline disaster weeks or months before they happened. In Cincinnati, Ohio, David Booth's life was about to be turned upside down. Before May 1979, David had led an average life. He was married and raising a family. He had never had psychic-type dreams before. But one morning, he was jarred awake by a dream of an impending airline crash:

On the morning of May 16th, I had a dream. I'm looking out to my right over a field and there's this great big jet and it wasn't making the noise that it should. It wasn't a feeling of impending doom or that it was going to crash or anything. It just wasn't making the sound that it should. It just turns, with its wing up in the air, goes on its back and then it goes straight into the ground and explodes. When the explosion would begin to die out, that's when I would begin to wake up.

The next night he went to bed exhausted hoping that this night was more restful and that he wouldn't have the dream again. He dreamt it again and when he woke up, he discovered that he had been crying. The main feeling that he had was urgency. Feeling compelled to do something; to act.

As the week progressed and the dream repeated itself every night, David found it harder to ignore but still kept the dream to himself.

Tuesday, May 22nd, David had the dream for the seventh night in a row. He felt that he could have no peace until he did something. David contacted the Cincinnati office of the Federal Aviation Administration and spoke to facilities manager, Paul Williams who reported:

> The first thing David described to me was the type of aircraft he thought it was. First of all he identified it as an American Airlines plane. I asked him if he knew specifically what type of aircraft it was but David didn't know one type of aircraft from another.

Williams asked David to search his dream in an effort to try to retrieve more information about the type of aircraft or any other details he could remember. But each night it came back frustratingly the same. All that week they spent hours reviewing the details. He described an aeroplane with an engine on the tail rather than in the tail and Williams identified that as a DC-10.

At the start of the Memorial Day weekend, David had the dream for the tenth time. Somehow he knew he would never have the dream again. He was on the brink of a nervous collapse and went home early that day. It was 4 o'clock; 3 o'clock at Chicago's O'Hare Airport.

When Williams had received the news from Chicago, he was sure that what David Booth had described to him before had actually come to pass. After David found out what had happened, he emotionally just fell apart. He immediately telephoned Paul Williams. Williams said that he believed that David was blaming himself for not getting enough information soon enough to avert the disaster. Williams, however, assured him that he had done everything that he could have.

Was David's dream actually about the ill-fated crash of Flight 191? All the facts seemed to add up including how the plane banked sharply to its left after losing an engine to nose-diving soon after takeoff. Even the type and brand of airline was correct. It is William's opinion that David was chosen to receive this dream for some reason known only to God.

The Aberfan disaster was a catastrophic collapse of a colliery spoil tip in the Welsh village of Aberfan, near Merthyr Tydfil, on 21 October 1966, killing 116 children and 28 adults. It was caused by a build-up of water in the accumulated rock and shale, which suddenly started to slide downhill in the form of slurry.

Over 40,000 cubic metres of debris covered the village in minutes, and the classrooms at Pantglas Junior School were immediately inundated, with young children and teachers dying from impact or suffocation. Many noted the poignancy of the situation: if the disaster had struck a few minutes earlier, the children would not have been in their classrooms, and if it had struck a few hours later, the school would have broken up for half-term.

Mrs. Lorna Middleton dreamed several nights in a row of children being buried in a cave-in.

One of the strangest cases of a precognitive dream happened to the writer Rudyard Kipling. In his memoir, *Something of Myself*, he tells the following story:

I dreamt that I stood, in my best clothes, which I do not wear as a rule, one in a line of similarly habited men, in some vast hall, floored with rough-jointed stone slabs. Opposite me, the width of the hall, was another line of persons and the impression of a crowd behind them. On my left some ceremony was taking place that I wanted to see, but could not unless I stepped out of my line because the fat stomach of my neighbour on my left barred my vision. At the ceremony's close, both lines of spectators broke up and moved forward and met, and the great space filled with people. Then a man came up behind me, slipped his hand beneath my arm, and said: "I want a word with you." I forget the rest but it had been a perfectly clear dream, and it stuck in my memory. Six weeks or more later, I attended in my capacity as a Member of the War Graves Commission a ceremony at Westminster Abbey, where the Prince of Wales dedicated a plaque to The Million Dead of the Great War. We commissioners lined up facing, across the width of the Abbey Nave, more members of the Ministry, and a big body of the public behind them, all in black clothes. I could see nothing of the ceremony because the stomach of the man on my left barred my vision. Then, my eye was caught by the cracks of the stone flooring, and I said to myself: "But here is where I have been!" We broke up, both lines flowed forward and met, and the Nave filled with a crowd, through which a man came up and slipped his hand upon my arms saying: "I want a word with you, please." It was about some utterly trivial matter that I have forgotten.

But how, and why, had I been shown an unreleased roll of my life-film?

My father, who was born in 1894, and was brought up in the Congregational Church, told me the following story when I was thirteen. It closely resembles Rudyard Kipling's dream in that the details of the dream are reproduced exactly in the fulfilment. This and other similar stories have helped me to draw the conclusions about precognition that I will outline in another chapter, namely that, in some way, we cannot understand, there is a life-film that unwinds as we go along. All of the future is somehow imprinted on that life-film and some people are able to see a preview of it in dreams and through mediums and psychics.

My father was friends with a Rev. and Mrs. Camp. Rev. Camp was a Congregational minister. In 1920 Mrs. Camp had a very vivid dream which she told to many people. She dreamt her husband died while preaching and that she had made her way through a great crowd of people to find him dying behind velvet curtains. The dream made a deep impression on her; she often felt anxious when her husband was preaching, but could never understand the velvet curtains.

On November 12, 1925, a full five years after the dream, her husband was asked to give the address at the Armistice Service in the Pier Pavilion. There were 2,500 persons present and she sat with her daughter at the back of the hall. As she was finding the last hymn someone said, "Your husband has fainted." She looked up and saw her husband being carried from the platform. She made her way through the crowd and when she got on the platform she found her husband lying dead behind green velvet drop curtains.

This case is fully corroborated by people who were told about the dream before the fulfilling event took place. The detail of the velvet curtains presents a knotty obstacle in the way of too-glib attempts to explain precognition. Are we to suppose that Reverend Camp was destined not only to die while preaching, but also to die behind velvet curtains?

A Spanish man related the following story to me about dreaming future events that happened in great detail:

I'm going to start recording every single one of my dreams from now on, because I experienced something inexplicable. I had a premonition in my dream where I experienced many COMPLETE EVENTS in my FUTURE. When I woke up from this dream, I had a "sense" that everything was going to happen, sometime in the future. I don't expect anyone AT ALL to believe me, but this is what happened: I literally dreamed for what felt like a month in dreamworld. When I woke up, it felt like I had awakened from a rather lengthy hibernation, when in reality, I slept about 12 hours. I only vividly recall the first weekend of my dream, where I had attended a graduation party with my friends' family. In my dream, I went to the party, I drove with a friend, came back to the party, played ping pong and beer pong the whole night, went to sleep. The family took my car keys so that I wouldn't drive home. The very next day, I went to go pick up my car, then my friends and I went to play soccer. We ate at a place called Liberty Burger then I drove home. I listened to the radio on my way back, but decided to take a joy ride around the city with music blasted just for good fun.

Now, here's the spooky part, the part that could get me thrown into a mental institution ...

I EXPERIENCED all of those events exactly, and I mean 100% EXACTLY as they happened in my dream, just a few weeks after. I'm not sure if there's anybody that can relate, because it wasn't just some random déjà-vu; it was as if I had written my own story, and then acted it out without my complete awareness of the situation. Every single freaking detail was correct ... every face I saw was the same, every car on the street ... every CONVERSATION was the same ... every physical movement (I predicted exactly how I would make the last ping pong/beer pong shot). I predicted that I would spill a drink at a restaurant ... every colour was the same ... every song on the radio played in the same exact sequence. I knew it was going to rain in the morning ... the clothes on everyone exactly the same ... the routes taken in the car. My ALMOST flat tyre ... I lost a lighter ... I even wrote a book title. And that's not even all of what happened! There's too much and I literally could write a book about my experiences.

The following story was related to me by a friend who is now deceased, and goes on to further illustrate the idea of a dream previewing part of a person's life-film, inasmuch as all of the details of the dream are eventually reproduced in the fulfilment.

The dreamer, in this case, was my late friend's wife, Maria. The dream was a very colourful scene of a jetty surrounded by intensely blue water, a background of rocky shore. Maria viewed the scene from the point of view of the jetty itself. The chief interest, however, lay in the fact that two sailors, whom Maria judged to be French because of the red pom-poms on their caps, were leaning over a nearby railing, so placed that they were almost facing Maria, and looking out over the water. The dream was so strong as to become permanently stamped on her memory.

The fulfilment came about on September 12, 1955 when Maria and her husband were on a three-week visit to Toronto. One afternoon Maria decided to go to the Zoo. She went by ferry boat and having spent an interesting afternoon there, walked into the jetty to board the return ferry boat. Being too early, she sat on the jetty covering her eyes from the very bright sunlight. Suddenly, on glancing toward the shore, she received quite a shock to see the picture of her prevision in the dream, in exact detail, with the two French sailors, red pom-poms and all, leaning over the rail exactly as they had been doing in her dream.

Pursuing the life-film theory a little further (and there are countless examples of this in a chapter to come) the following story about an actress who dreamt her acting roles years before the scripts had been written or even conceived serves to strengthen my case.

From 1954 to 1965, a period of eleven years, Christine Mylius had 1,300 precognitive dreams, which were studied by Professor Hans Bender at the University of Freiburg in Germany. Among these were several in which she dreamed of scenes in a film she was to act in two years later. At this time she had no knowledge of such a film and what her part would be in it.

The film, *Night Fell upon Gotenhafen*, went into production late in 1959. In the movie a group of farm women fought their way to a ship in the seaport of Gotenhafen, near Danzig, during World War II. The ship was hit by Russian torpedoes in the Baltic Sea, and most of the refugees were drowned.

On September 15, 1957, two years before the first scenes of the film were shot, and before the script was even written, Mrs. Mylius had what Dr. Bender called her "baby" dream. In this dream she was swimming with several women and their babies when one of the babies swam underwater, and Mrs. Mylius was afraid the child would die. In a scene from the picture filmed two years later, the farm woman played by Mrs. Mylius had a newborn child. The baby died during the torpedoing, and Mrs. Mylius then jumped from a lifeboat into the water.

On October 10, 1957, Mrs. Mylius had her "swimming" dream. A cameraman was trying to photograph her as she swam but she refused, thinking, "It is not worth it." In the actual film, two years later, the character played by Mrs. Mylius was drowned when she leaped into the water during the torpedoing. As Mrs. Mylius sank beneath the surface, pulled down by a diver outside camera range, an underwater camera recorded her descent. The sequence was filmed three times, leaving the actress in a state of exhaustion. The scene was later cut from the film, and the dream had correctly predicted that Mrs. Mylius's effort was indeed "not worth it".

On April 29, 1958 – about a year and a half before the first scenes were shot – Mrs. Mylius had her "ship's cook" dream. In the dream it was early evening and she was on a small ocean steamer. The passengers were resting in deck chairs, and she was having a "pleasant and animated" conversation with the ship's cook.

One evening in September 1959, during the filming at sea, Mrs. Mylius was reminded of this dream. It was very hot, and the actors and crew were lying on deck chairs on the steamer, which was actually a chartered fishing boat. Mrs. Mylius sat next to an actor who had recently introduced her to a friend of his, the ship's cook. The latter was a kindly man who attended to Mrs Mylius whenever she would come on the boat exhausted after hours of swimming in the sea.

The fishing boat itself appeared in a dream on May 22, 1959. The dreamer was on a "very old, dirty steamer" which was difficult to manoeuvre and took hours to get out of port. The crew was "unkempt" and "somewhat drunk". In the film the actual fishing boat, loaded with coal, was very old and dirty. The members of the real-life crew drank continually. And it was several hours before the boat finally got out of Bremerhaven to begin its film journey.

In February and July, 1958, Mrs Mylius dreamed about a "gigantic lobster with huge claws, which was eaten at a great feast, party with many people." During the filming the divers, hired for the shipwreck scenes, caught a large lobster weighing almost twelve pounds. Mrs. Myiius prepared a lobster dinner for "a party with many people".

One of the divers, a girl, appeared earlier in Mrs. Mylius's dreams. On January 3, 1959, Mrs. Mylius dreamed of "protective asbestos suits", "a crater filled with a white chalky substance" and a picture of a woman with flowing hair.

Each element of this dream came true during the filming. On the first day after the company's arrival in Heligoland, the actors tried a new type of protective asbestos suit to prevent drowning. A "crater lake" composed of a white, chalky substance had been formed along the jetty of Heligoland. One of the divers, an attractive girl named Evelyn, with flowing hair, bore a striking resemblance to the girl in the dream-portrait.

It should be born in mind that the script had not even been written when Mrs. Mylius began dreaming about the film and her role in it Nor was it even certain which scenes would be filmed. At the time of the "boat" dream, three months before the filming began, there was no plan to charter a fishing boat.

As you will soon discover in the chapter on psychics and mediums who predict the future, it is my view that these events have already happened in some strange way, already formed and taken shape at the time of the precognitive dream. This is the only possible explanation if the events are fulfilled later.

When I was twenty-eight years old I began having dreams about working in a large, sandy coloured building. In the dream, there was no clue as to the location of the building. In one dream I saw a classic motor car which looked like a Rolls Royce being pushed up a ramp and into the building through a large door. In the summer of 1980, while working at public television station WGBH in Boston, I saw a classic Rolls Royce being driven up a ramp in the parking lot of the building to be used on the set of *Masterpiece Theater*; the WGBH building, which was then located on Western Avenue in Boston, was a sandy coloured building.

My friend, Alex Tanous, told me the following story of how a dream helped him solve a police case. When an eight-year-old boy disappeared from his home in Freeport, Maine (and was later found suffocated) Alex sketched a murder suspect for the police from a dream in which he saw the boy, with no knowledge of his identity. Alex had been consulted at the request of the boy's parents and relatives. The Freeport police chief, Herman Boudreau, was concentrating on four key suspects at the time and wished to see if Alex's sketch would match any of the four people he had in mind. After giving several clues, Alex produced a sketch of the man he felt was the culprit. It tallied with the description, which the police possessed but did not reveal, of Milton Wallace.

The police chief took a chance and decided to accuse the suspect of the crime. Alex had been right all along. Wallace confessed to the crime.

Carl Jung, who we met in Chapter One, recounts in *Memories, Dreams, Reflections* of a vivid dream he had of a deceased friend:

One night I lay awake thinking of the sudden death of a friend whose funeral had taken place the day before. I was deeply concerned. Suddenly I dreamt that he was in the room. It seemed to me that he stood at the foot of my bed and was asking me to go with him. I did not have the feeling on an apparition; rather, it was an inner visual image of him, which I explained to myself as a fantasy. But in all honesty I had to ask myself, "Do I have any proof that this is

149

a fantasy? Suppose it is not a fantasy, suppose my friend is really here and I decided he was only a fantasy – would that not be abominable of me?" Yet I had equally little proof that he stood before me as an apparition. Then I said to myself, "Proof is neither here nor there! Instead of explaining him away as a fantasy I might just as well give him the benefit of the doubt and for experiment's sake credit him with reality." The moment I had that thought, he went to the door and beckoned me to follow him.

He led me out of the house, into the garden, out to the road, and finally to his house. I went in, and he conducted me into his study. He climbed on a stool and showed me the second of five books with red bindings which stood on the second shelf from the top. Then the dream broke off. I was not familiar with his library and did not know what books he owned. Certainly I could never have made out from below the titles of the books he had pointed out to me on the second shelf from the top.

This experience seemed to me so curious that next morning I went to his widow and asked whether I could look up something in my friend's library. Sure enough, there was a stool standing under the bookcase I had seen in my dream, and even before I came closer I could see the five books with the red bindings. I stepped up on the stool so as to be able to read the titles. They were translations of the novels of Emile Zola. The title of the second volume read, *The Legacy of the Dead*. The contents seemed to be of no interest. Only the title was extremely significant in connection with this experience.

So what of dreams? What can we make of a dream in which we see events that happen weeks, months or even years in the future? These kinds of dreams, along with most other things in this book, simply point to a different picture of how the universe works.

F. W. H. Myers

Alex Tanous

Edgar Cayce

Carl Jung

Ed and Lorraine Warren

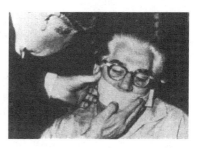

Leslie Flint

Chapter Eight

Ghosts I've Met

I subscribe to the atmospheric photograph theory. It may be that all our actions, and everything that happens are recorded on some sort of eternal tape, and under certain conditions, maybe climatic conditions, in the presence of certain people occasionally they reappear. I don't honestly think that the figures that are seen represent an afterlife.
Peter Underwood

On the popular American television show, *Ghost Hunters*, a crew of self-appointed psychic researchers travel the back roads of America looking for ghosts, hauntings, and everything spectral. You seldom see anything visual on the show that would actually resemble a ghost. The "investigators" are really a pair of plumbers moonlighting as ghostbusters for clients who report paranormal phenomena. Jason Hawes and Grant Wilson founded TAPS, The Atlantic Paranormal Society, in 1990 as an extension of their interest in the paranormal, and since that time they have made it their life's work – when they're not unclogging drains, that is – to help individuals or groups throughout the country who feel they have been affected by seemingly unexplained disturbances. Grant left TAPS and the show in 2012, leaving Jason as the team's lead investigator.

One of my criticisms of the show is that they refuse to use a medium on their investigations, such as medium Peter James was used on the old *Sightings* show.

Another similar show is the UK's *Most Haunted*. The TV show that has spooked millions with its footage of hauntings and poltergeists has been exposed as a fake by one its own stars.

Resident parapsychologist Dr Ciaran O'Keeffe has

sensationally lifted the lid on the ghost-hunting series, *Most Haunted* ... and claims that the public are being deceived by "showmanship and dramatics".

He accuses the show's medium Derek Acorah of hoodwinking viewers by pretending to communicate with spirits and obtaining information about locations prior to filming.

The Mirror newspaper has also obtained unedited footage which appears to show presenter Yvette Fielding and her husband faking 'paranormal' occurrences such as ghostly bumps and knocks.

Most Haunted has quickly achieved cult status since it was launched in 2002 and is LivingTV's most successful programme.

Millions of viewers tuned in regularly to watch Ex-Blue Peter girl Yvette and her team of ghost hunters spend the night in some of Britain's most haunted locations.

It made Acorah – who claims to be guided by an Ethiopian spirit guide called Sam – into one of the country's best-known psychics.

Whether genuine or faked, these kinds of programmes rarely, if ever, subscribe to any theory other than the one that a deceased person is "haunting" the premises. And yet, it is my view that 90% of all hauntings are replays on some kind of etheric film, of a past even, what Peter Underwood called the atmospheric photograph theory. Psychical researcher Harry Price called these kinds of hauntings "etheric memories". He spoke in some detail about this to George Woods and Betty Green in a 1963 Leslie Flint direct voice séance:

First I think we must accept the fact that scientific proof, proof that would be accepted purely on scientific grounds is not likely to come. Science is only concerned with one hundred per cent proof. The reason for my coming is that I thought a discussion, a talk, on ghosts, would be interesting, and also perhaps answer certain questions in regard to them. One often hears of ghosts and entities that haunt a certain place, often for centuries. And sometimes they are, according to the mentality of the ghost in question, a nuisance and sometimes they are undesirable from the point of view that they disturb and frighten individuals that happen to be living on the premises. There are various kinds of ghosts. First you have the ghost of an individual, perhaps long since dead that has no connection with the actual spirit of the person concerned. You may have a very powerful thought force which may, by its very power, give the impression that the individual person or personality is there on the occasion of the haunting. And there are people who when they have seen what they term to be a ghost are under the impression that they have seen, in outward shape and form, the individual who has long since been dead. What is actually happening is the individual concerned is not necessarily present. It is an astral projection on the atmosphere which on certain occasions usually when the atmosphere is conducive to it, manifests itself. But this apparition has no power whatsoever because the mentality, the mind of the ghost is not there, it's not present. In other words it is a kind of a shell that is formed out of the ether under certain conditions. It has a limited power. It can only move in certain areas, and can only been seen by people who are, without realizing it, mediumistic inasmuch as they can see onto that vibration which is all around the earth. A ghost is just a very strong thought vibration which has impregnated itself on the atmosphere in a certain place, invariably because at the time of the death of the individual their thoughts were so strong that they left behind a memory condition which can be to some extent tangible. It has no condition with the individual. It is a condition of the past which has registered itself very strongly on the atmosphere thereby being able to recreate shape and substance of a kind which has no physical power but is merely an etheric condition. You find that in very old houses and castles that these apparitions do appear. It is very common. People need to realize that the astral world which does link up with yours is in a sense a mirror. It registers and is able to show all manner of incidents pertaining to man's life, particularly at the point of death.

The earth world is surrounded, completely and absolutely, by this etheric condition of life or substance such as it is which contains reflections of past events. In fact, one might say that anything that has happened of any consequence individually and collectively to man, is still in the atmosphere.

With poltergeists it is completely different. Usually you will find someone in the household who is full of vitality and power and psychic force that makes it possible for them to use the power drawn from the individual in the household to move furniture or to throw things about. The reason is that they invariably wish for something in that house to be discovered. It may be money that is hidden, or it could be a body which perhaps has been buried under the floorboards. There are many reasons why some spirits do return and haunt places because they want something put right. They cannot rest in their new environment. They are concerned with material things and until that something is put right they feel that they cannot leave the earth world without this matter being settled. Often a person will die leaving money hidden someplace and they feel that they should have left a will. There are all manner of things that cause people to be earthbound. Usually the person is not earthbound for a very long time because if after a period of time they are not able to get in touch they begin to realize the futility of trying.

Then there are apparitions of dogs, of horses, of cats, even of birds. These apparitions are not necessarily real from the point of view that the soul is present. These come under the category of etheric manifestations which are thought forms on the ether which at certain times are visible. These cases of horse drawing carriages have no real substance. They become a reality inasmuch that they are definitely seen and witnessed by people on your side but they have no real substance. They are etheric reproductions of events that have taken place hundreds of years ago:

Very little is known about this. There are people in your world, clergymen, who think they are performing exorcisms. No one has the power to exorcise ghosts. Most churchmen in your world have no idea what comes after death. Sometimes a haunting may be deliberate inasmuch as it may bring in the clergyman and make him try to do something about it, but much more important to make him think more seriously about it, to try and make him know there is something in the truth of survival. A lot of things that go on and are perhaps a little bewildering are deliberately done to make people realize that there is something outside of your normal everyday existence. If we can bring the Church into it and make them think more seriously about life after death and communication between the two worlds as well, then we are doing a good job. You know, we use all manner of ways to try to bring the truth of survival to the world. And hauntings are to us a way of arousing interest.

BG: Are there not some people who are simply earthbound because they know nothing about an afterlife?

HP: There are people who are earthbound because of ignorance and because they are so much held down by material thoughts. I am afraid this is bound to be. At any rate I hope I have shed some light on the subject of ghosts. I must go. Goodbye.

Harry Price's comment about the spirit of a person returning for reasons such as money under the floorboards is dramatically pointed out in what has become known as the Chaffin will case. A North Carolina farmer, James Chaffin, had died leaving his farm to his third son and nothing to his wife and other three sons. But Chaffin had made a later will, one which divided the property equally between his wife and the other sons, and had hidden it away.

In June 1925 the youngest son, James, dreamed that his father stood by his bedside, attired in an old black overcoat, and told him, "You will find the will in my overcoat pocket." The following morning Chaffin hurried to his mother and asked about his father's old overcoat; She told him it had been given to his brother John. He found the coat at John's house and examined it carefully. Sewn into the lining of the inside pocket, which his father had indicated in the dream, he found a roll of paper stating: "Read the 27th chapter of Genesis in my daddy's old Bible."

Taking a neighbour as a witness, Chaffin went back to his mother's house and turned up the Bible. In the 27th chapter of Genesis there was another will, made later than the one that left everything to his brother Marshall, dividing the property equally. Ten witnesses testified to the fact that it was in old James Chaffin's handwriting.

The Chaffin will case tallies exactly with my late friend Alex Tanous's explanation of ghosts:

I, like many people, believe that ghosts exist because they must tell their story to someone who can set their lives and actions into balance. I agree, however, that it will always be a metaphysical question as to why ghosts appear. If, as some religions promise, existence after death is a happy and fulfilling experience in the vastness of eternity, why would an apparition choose to limit itself to our world? Is the entity progressing towards some sort of consciousness? Are apparitions simply imprinted energy fields rooted to a particularly charged intense emotional incident like the shadowed after-image of an atomic blast?

It is my belief that the entity is, in fact, moving forward in its own consciousness, but at times has the ability to return for the sole purpose of balancing human events or human injustice in experiences where they lived. At the appropriate time the entity can create an apparition (or related phenomena: movements, bangs and raps, etc.) whose aim it is to restore the universe to harmony, including his or her own individuality within the wholeness of the universe. This can be done in any way the entity sees fit, because both the cause and the concept of the injustice began with the entity itself. From there, I feel it is up to the overriding consciousness of the apparition to decide what it wants to do about a given situation and how it wants to convey its cry for help and understanding. Sometimes, in begging for help, an entity will cause horrible things to happen, such as poltergeist activity directed at people.

A common cause of any appearance of an apparition is when another person tries to restore or change a setting or house by adding an extra wing to the building, dividers to a room, a wall to demarcate property – anything that represents physical change. In these instances the entity doesn't understand it is now in a different dimension and resents the fact that its world is being altered to suit the needs of other people.

Ghosts will often haunt a location where they feel an injustice has been done, in a frail attempt to balance the cosmos and restore harmony to the universe through the attempts of the living to intervene for them and the perceived cause. Ghosts will also manifest if the situation of the living people in the house or site at all resembles the situation in which the ghost found itself before death. For example, ghosts who had mourned the death of children during life will often attach themselves to living children in the house. In other cases, if a promise has been broken, a ghost will manifest itself in order to remind the living that they have responsibilities to keep their promises, even to people who have long since died.

And there are cases in which a ghost will manifest out of a simple love of life. Sometime during the early 1980s, at a summer seminar held at a small college in New England, I was showing another psychic around a lake on campus. Both of us saw a little girl playing with two dogs. As we watched, the little girl rushed into the bushes and came out moments later followed only by the larger dog. After asking around, we discovered that the small dog once belonged to a student. The dog had died but it came back to the lake because it loved to play.

One of the most interesting (and disturbing) incidents of me meeting a ghost took place in the 1960s in the radio studio where I worked as an announcer in Norfolk, Virginia. The station was all-classical WRVC-FM and it was housed in a very old building in an old section of Norfolk. One morning, while I was preparing the news for broadcast, I heard what sounded like scraping sounds coming from behind the transmitter. I got up and walked around the transmitter to see if anything was there. There wasn't. The sounds continued however and were so loud that it interfered with me announcing the music. Around an hour later the noises abruptly stopped, interestingly just before the office staff arrived for work for the day. When I related the incident to the station manager he suggested that I cut back on the booze. I was used to the electrical and mechanical sounds that issued from the room just outside the booth. The news teletype machine making a sort of hammering noise as it ground out the paper on which the news was printed. One morning, I failed to notice that the noise was continuing longer than usual. When I walked out into the room, there were reams of teletype paper all over the floor.

Another incident was more startling, and falls into the "atmospheric photograph theory" put forward by Peter

Underwood. I was living in a very old house at the time on a cobblestone street. This must have been around 1972. The house was built sometime after 1890. I was told that it had been the home and office of a doctor named Grandy. One night I was sitting in the library of the house reading a book. I got up to get a glass of brandy. As I turned the corner to go into the kitchen, I saw the figure of a man carrying a doctor's bag. He was stooped over. He walked right through a door and into a closet. He appeared perfectly solid. Upon enquiring, I later learned that the door where the closet was now located had once been the door.

In the summer of 1989 I was working at WGBH/Boston, the flagship PBS station that produces the best programmes America has to offer. One day I had an extremely interesting encounter with William Pierce. Bill was the silver-toned announcer for the Boston Symphony Orchestra broadcasts which were heard nationwide. He was also the TV booth announcer for WGBH-TV. Bill walked into my office and sat on my desk and told me he had a proposition for me. He asked me if I would like to be an announcer on WGBH TV, part time, inasmuch as he could not be at Symphony Hall and also do the TV booth announcing. The job entailed doing station breaks and announcements for upcoming shows. Bill explained that he had set it up with the head of television for me to have the part-time job and that he would train me. We sat side by side in a small booth and I learned how to take my cues from the engineer who was on the other side of the glass. The next week I was on my own. Near midnight, just before sign-off I noticed a strange presence in the booth. It was as though there was someone in the booth with me. And yet I was totally alone. This phenomenon repeated itself several times. I never did discover what it was.

Stephen King and his wife spent a night at the Stanley Hotel in Estes Park, Co., in late September 1974. Because the resort was to be closed for the winter the very next day, the writer and his wife were the only guests in the sprawling hotel, which King would later describe as the archetypal setting for a ghost story. Legend has it that King stayed in room 217, where he saw the spirit of a young boy in distress, but according to the writer's official website, it was a vivid dream of his own 3-year-old son running terrified through the corridors that jolted King awake that night and helped to inspire his classic horror story, *The Shining*.

According to some accounts, King and his wife put their suitcases in room 217 after checking in then left the room for dinner. They returned to find all their belongings neatly put away, but not by any living member of the hotel staff. Despite the famous link between room 217 and one of the scariest novels of all time, many visitors believe room 401 actually boasts the most paranormal activity. Guests staying here have reported hearing the sounds of children running and playing in the halls when no children were present, the feeling of blankets being pulled tight across legs and feet, and even the sensation of the bed gently shaking as they slept. The ghosts of F.O. Stanley and his wife Flora, who built the hotel in 1909, are said to frequent the bar and billiards areas and the ballroom, where Flora's piano sometimes plays all by itself.

While alleged ghost sightings at the Stanley Hotel are certainly frequent, they don't seem to be particularly threatening or violent, which may help to account for the popularity of the ghost tours still led by the management of this stately hotel.

While living in London in 1999, I travelled to Cheltenham to investigate a haunting that also falls into the category of the atmospheric photograph theory. The story is that of an old woman who is seen crossing the road. I interviewed several of the people living in that area who claimed to have witnessed her.

On a cold day in 1989 Mrs. Jackson, an assistant cook who lives in Woodmancote, Bishop's Cleve, Cheltenham, was having a driving-lesson. Her instructor was seated to her left, in the front of the car. As she approached the corner of Pittville

Circus Road and All Saints Road, Cheltenham, a tall woman in black, with her hand held to her face, stepped into the path of the car. When Mrs. Jackson braked, her instructor asked her for the reason. She replied that there was a woman in plain sight crossing the road in front of the car; he responded, "I can see pink elephants too." When Mrs. Jackson looked back again, the woman had disappeared.

In mid-July 1985 a middle-aged musician was walking with a friend in the vicinity of the Pittville Circus Road. It was about ten o'clock in the evening. Suddenly, about seventy yards away, they spotted the figure of a woman with her left hand held up to her face, wearing a long black dress of the type worn in the 1880s. He reported that, "She was walking, seemingly gliding along the path towards the corner." The woman stopped, turned around and looked straight at the couple. When he waved to her, she "moved to the centre of the pathway, still glancing in our direction". I note that she did not wave back. Apparently frightened, the couple decided not to approach any closer, and they proceeded with their walk. When they later changed their mind and returned to the spot, the woman had vanished.

The same man saw the apparition again that August. This time it was around midnight, and he was driving along the Pitville Circus Road when he saw the same woman crossing the road about ten yards in front of him. She was gliding again in the direction of a driveway of a large empty house on the opposite side of the road. The man told me that he distinctly saw that the woman had her left hand held to her face with a handkerchief. He estimated that she was in full view for about twenty-five minutes.

The 'Cheltenham Haunting' or 'Morton Ghost' as it is often described first came to public attention in 1892 when an account was published in the Journal of the SPR under the title 'Record of a Haunted House'.

This was partly at the instigation of Frederick W.H. Myers,

one of the founders of the SPR who was then currently living in Cheltenham and after hearing an account of the haunting became interested in the case. The identity of the family concerned and the location of the house itself were concealed when the haunting first came to light, the SPR paper being written by a 'Miss R.C. Morton'. It was not until 1948 when all the principal witnesses were dead that the basic facts of the case were published for the first time.

Myers became involved in 1884 when the haunting was in progress and had actually reached what was to be its peak. Principal phenomena lasted in total for a period of seven years from 1882 to 1889 although there is a body of evidence for it continuing for periods until relatively recent times. In the main, the haunting comprised the appearance of the figure of a tall woman dressed in black invariably with her features partly concealed by a handkerchief held up to the lower part of her face. This combined with the dark clothing gave the apparition the appearance of someone wearing 'widow's weeds' or at least in the aspect of mourning.

I have made an intensive study of the haunting of Borley Rectory, the subject of Harry Price's book about what he called the most haunted house in England. Borley Rectory in Essex, built in 1862, should have been an ordinary Victorian clergyman's house. However, just a year after its construction, unexplained footsteps were heard within the house, and from 1900 until it burned down in 1939 numerous paranormal phenomena, including phantom coaches and shattering windows, were observed. In 1929 the house was investigated by the *Daily Mail* and paranormal researcher Harry Price, and it was he who called it 'the most haunted house in England'. Price also took out a lease on the rectory from 1937 to 1938, recruiting forty-eight 'official observers' to monitor occurrences. After his death in 1948, the water was muddied by claims that Price's findings were not genuine paranormal activity, and ever since there has been a debate over what really went on at Borley Rectory.

The first paranormal events reportedly occurred in about 1863, since a few locals later remembered having heard unexplained footsteps within the house at about that time. On 28 July 1900, four daughters of the rector, Henry Dawson Ellis Bull, saw what they thought was the ghost of a nun at twilight, about 40 yards (37 m) from the house; they tried to talk to it, but it disappeared as they got closer. The local organist recalled that the family at the rectory were "very convinced that they had seen an apparition on several occasions". [Various people claimed to have witnessed a variety of puzzling incidents, such as a phantom coach driven by two headless horsemen, during the next four decades.] Henry Dawson Ellis Bull died in 1892 and his son, the Reverend Henry ("Harry") Foyster Bull, took over the living.

On 9 June 1928, Henry ("Harry") Bull died and the rectory again became vacant. In the following year, on 2 October, the Reverend Guy Eric Smith and his wife moved into the house. Soon after moving in Mrs Smith, while cleaning out a cupboard, came across a brown paper package containing the skull of a young woman. Shortly after, the family reported a variety of incidents including the sounds of servant bells ringing despite their being disconnected, lights appearing in windows and unexplained footsteps. In addition, Mrs Smith believed she saw a horse-drawn carriage at night. The Smiths contacted the *Daily Mirror* asking to be put in touch with the Society for Psychical Research (SPR). On 10 June 1929 the newspaper sent a reporter, who promptly wrote the first in a series of articles detailing the mysteries of Borley. The paper also arranged for Harry Price, a paranormal researcher, to make his first visit to the house that would ultimately make him famous. He arrived on 12 June and immediately phenomena of a new kind appeared, such as the throwing of stones, a vase and other objects. "Spirit messages" were tapped out from the frame of a mirror. As soon as Harry

Price left, these ceased. Mrs Smith later maintained that she already suspected Price, an expert conjurer, of falsifying the phenomena.

The Smiths left Borley on 14 July 1929, and the parish had some difficulty in finding a replacement. The following year the Reverend Lionel Algernon Foyster (1878–1945), a first cousin of the Bulls, and his wife Marianne (née Marianne Emily Rebecca Shaw) (1899–1992) moved into the rectory with their adopted daughter Adelaide, on 16 October 1930. Lionel Foyster wrote an account of various strange incidents that occurred between the time the Foysters moved in and October 1935, which was sent to Harry Price. These included bell-ringing, windows shattering, throwing of stones and bottles, wall-writing, and the locking of their daughter in a room with no key. Marianne Foyster reported to her husband a whole range of poltergeist phenomena that included her being thrown from her bed. On one occasion, Adelaide was attacked by "something". Foyster tried twice to conduct an exorcism, but his efforts were fruitless; in the middle of the first exorcism, he was struck in the shoulder by a fist-size stone. Because of the publicity in the *Daily Mirror*, these incidents attracted the attention of several psychic researchers, who after investigation were unanimous in suspecting that they were caused, consciously or unconsciously, by Marianne Foyster. Mrs Foyster later stated that she felt that some of the incidents were caused by her husband in concert with one of the psychic researchers, but other events appeared to her to be genuine paranormal phenomena. Marianne later admitted that she was having a sexual relationship with the lodger, Frank Pearless, and that she used paranormal explanations to cover up her liaisons. The Foysters left Borley in October 1935 as a result of Lionel's ill health.

Borley remained vacant for some time after the Foysters' departure, until in May 1937 Price took out a year-long rental agreement with Queen Anne's Bounty, the owners of the property.

Through an advertisement in *The Times* on 25 May 1937 and subsequent personal interviews, Price recruited a corps of 48 "official observers", mostly students, who spent periods, mainly during weekends, at the rectory with instructions to report any phenomena that occurred. In March 1938 Helen Glanville (the daughter of S. J. Glanville, one of Price's helpers) conducted a planchette séance in Streatham in South London. Price reported that she made contact with two spirits, the first of which was that of a young nun who identified herself as Marie Lairre. According to the planchette story Marie was a French nun who left her religious order and travelled to England to marry a member of the Waldegrave family, the owners of Borley's seventeenth-century manor house, Borley Hall. She was said to have been murdered in an earlier building on the site of the rectory, and her body either buried in the cellar or thrown into a disused well. The wall writings were alleged to be her pleas for help; one read "Maria". On 27 February 1939 the new owner of the rectory, Captain W. H. Gregson, was unpacking boxes and accidentally knocked over an oil lamp in the hallway. The fire quickly spread and the house was severely damaged. After investigating the cause of the blaze the insurance company concluded that the fire had been started deliberately.

Miss Williams from nearby Borley Lodge said she saw the figure of the ghostly nun in the upstairs window and, according to Harry Price, demanded a fee of one guinea for her story. In August 1943 Harry Price conducted a brief dig in the cellars of the ruined house and discovered two bones thought to be of a young woman.

I was always fascinated with the alleged haunting of the Queen Mary, moored up at Long Beach, California. During my time in Los Angeles, I visited the Queen Mary many times. It has now been turned into a hotel and a sort of living museum of the past.

Internationally recognized, the historic floating hotel and museum attracts thousands of visitors every year. It has also attracted a number of unearthly guests over the years. In fact, some say the Queen Mary is one of the most haunted places in the world with as many as 150 known spirits lurking upon the ship. Over the past 60 years, the Queen Mary has been the site of at least 49 reported deaths, not to mention having gone through the terrors of war, so it comes as no surprise that spectral spirits of her vivid past continue to walk within her rooms and hallways.

Located 50 feet below water level is the Queen Mary's engine room, which is said to be a hotbed of paranormal activity. Used in the filming of the Poseidon Adventure, the room's infamous "Door 13" crushed at least two men to death, at different points during the ship's history. The most recent death, during a routine watertight door drill in 1966, crushed an 18-year-old crew member. Dressed in blue coveralls and sporting a beard, the young man has often been spied walking the length of Shaft Alley before disappearing by door 13.

Two more popular spots for the Queen Mary's other worldly guests are its first- and second-class swimming pools. Though neither are utilized today for their original purpose, spirits seemingly are not aware of that. In the first-class swimming pool, which has been closed for more than three decades, women have often been seen appearing in 1930's style swimming suits wandering the decks near the pool. Others have reported the sounds of splashing and spied wet footprints leading from the deck to the changing rooms. Some have also spied the spirit of a young girl, clutching her teddy bear.

In the second-class poolroom, the spirit of another little girl named Jackie is often seen and heard. The unfortunate girl drowned in the pool during the ship's sailing days and reputedly refused to move on, as her voice, as well as the sounds of laughter has been captured here.

In the Queen's Salon, which once served as the ship's first-class lounge, a beautiful young woman in an elegant white evening gown has often been seen dancing alone in the shadows of the corner of the room.

Yet more odd occurrences have been made in a number of first-class staterooms. Here, reports have been made of a tall dark haired man appearing in a 1930's style suit, as well as water running and lights turning on in the middle of the night, and phones ringing in the early morning hours with no one on the other end of the line. In the third-class children's playroom, a baby's cry has often been heard, which is thought to be the infant boy who died shortly after his birth.

Other phenomena occurring throughout the ship, are the sounds of distinct knocks, doors slamming and high pitched squeals, drastic temperature changes, and the aromas of smells long past.

These are but a few of the many reports of apparitions and strange events.

Harry Price's explanation, in the Leslie Flint direct voice séance given to George Woods and Betty Greene of ghost horses, ghost dogs and even ghost buildings may just explain the following account given by an English couple of staying at a ghost hotel. My question on this case would be was their experience part of an etheric replay as Price discussed, or was it a time-slip, meaning did they actually go back in time. When I interviewed them they had no idea.

It all began innocently enough in October 1979, when two couples in Dover, England, set off on a vacation together, intending to travel through France and Spain. It ended in a journey that took them to another world.

Geoff and Pauline Simpson and their friends Len and Cynthia Gisby boarded a boat that took them across the English Channel to the coast of France. There, they rented a car and proceeded to drive north. Around 9:30 that evening, October 3, they began to tire and looked for a place to stay. They pulled off the autoroute when they saw a plush-looking motel.

Len went inside and in the lobby encountered a man dressed in an odd plum-coloured uniform. The man said there was no room in the motel but there was a small hotel south along the road. Len thanked him and he and his companions went on.

Along the way, they were struck by the oddness of the cobbled, narrow road and the buildings they passed. They also saw posters advertising a circus. "It was a very old-fashioned circus," Pauline would remember. "That's why we took so much interest."

Finally, the travellers saw a long, low building with a row of brightly lit windows. Some men were standing in front of it and when Cynthia spoke with them, they told her the place was an inn, not a hotel. They drove further down the road until they saw two buildings: one a police station, the other an old-fashioned two-story building bearing a sign marked "Hotel". Inside, everything was made of heavy wood. There were no tablecloths on the tables, nor was there any evidence of such modern conveniences as telephones or elevators.

The rooms were no less strange. The beds had heavy sheets and no pillows. There were no locks on the doors, only wooden catches. The bathroom the couples had to share had old-fashioned plumbing.

After they ate, they returned to their rooms and fell asleep. They were awakened when sunlight filtered through the windows, which consisted only of wooden shutters – no glass. They went back to the dining room and ate a simple breakfast with "black and horrible" coffee, Geoff recalled.

As they were sitting there, a woman wearing a silk evening gown and carrying a dog under her arm sat opposite them. "It was strange," Pauline told me. "It looked like she had just come in from a ball but it was seven in the morning. I couldn't take my eyes off her."

At that point, two gendarmes entered the room. "They were

nothing like the gendarmes we saw anywhere else in France," according to Geoff. "Their uniforms seemed to be very old." The uniforms were deep blue and the officers were wearing capes over their shoulders. Their hats were large and peaked.

Despite the oddities, the couples enjoyed themselves and, when they returned to their rooms, the two husbands separately took pictures of their wives standing by the shuttered windows.

On their way out, Len and Geoff talked with the gendarmes about the best way to take the autoroute to Avignon and the Spanish border. The officers didn't seem to understand the word "autoroute" and the travellers assumed they hadn't pronounced the French word properly. The directions they were given were quite poor; they took the friends to an old road some miles out of the way. They decided to use the map instead and take a more direct route along the highway. After the car was packed, Len went to pay his bill and was astonished when the manager asked only for 19 francs. Assuming there was some misunderstanding, Len explained that there were four of them and they had eaten a meal. The manager only nodded. Len showed the bill to the gendarmes, who smilingly indicated there was nothing amiss. He paid in cash and left before they could change their minds.

On their way back from two weeks in Spain, the two couples decided to stop at the hotel again. They had had a pleasant, interesting time there and the prices certainly couldn't be beaten. The night was rainy and cold and visibility poor, but they found the turnoff and noticed the circus signs they had seen before.

"This is definitely the right road," Pauline declared.

It was, but there was no hotel alongside it. Thinking that somehow they had missed it, they went back to the motel where the man in the plum-coloured suit had given them directions. That motel was there, but there was no man in the unusual suit and the clerk denied such an individual working there.

The couples drove three times up and down the road looking for something that, they were now beginning to realize, was no longer there.

They drove north and spent the night in a hotel in Lyons. A room with modern facilities, breakfast and dinner cost them 247 francs.

Upon their return to Dover, Geoff and Len had their respective rolls of film processed. In each case, the pictures of the hotel (one by Geoff, two by Len) were in the middle of the roll. But when they got the pictures back, the ones taken inside the hotel were missing. There were no spoiled negatives. Each film had its full quota of pictures. It was as if the pictures had never been taken except for one small detail that a reporter for Yorkshire television would notice: "There was evidence that the camera had tried to wind on in the middle of the film. Sprocket holes on the negatives showed damage."

The couples kept quiet about their experience for three years, telling it only to friends and family. One friend found a book in which it was revealed that gendarmes wore the uniforms described prior to 1905. Eventually, a reporter for the Dover newspaper heard the story and published an account. Later, a television dramatization of the experience was produced by a local station.

In 1985, Manchester psychiatrist Albert Keller hypnotized Geoff Simpson to see if he could recall any more of the peculiar event. Under hypnosis he added nothing new to what he consciously remembered.

This "ghost story" doesn't seem to fit into either the category of Harry Price's etheric replay or "live-action" ghost. What actually happened, nobody will probably ever know.

Celia Greene was the Director of the Institute for Psychophysical Research in Oxford, England. She spent twenty years studying reported cases of ghosts and apparitions.

Green has put forward the idea that lucid dreams, out-of-body experiences and apparitional experiences have something in common, namely that in all three types of case the subject's field of perception is entirely replaced by a hallucinatory one. In the first two types of case this is self-evident from the nature of the experience, but in the case of apparitional experiences in the waking state the idea is far from obvious. The hypothesis, and the evidence and arguments for it, were first put forward in her book *Apparitions*, and later developed in her book *Lucid Dreaming: the Paradox of Consciousness During Sleep*, both of which she co-authored with Charles McCreery. I cannot support the idea that Greene's subjects were hallucinating as it does not tie in with my own personal observations. The Warren Smith materialization séance which I attended as a teenager in which Carl Jung appeared was also attacked by the woman who took me there, Elba Hubbard, as mass hallucination, or mass hypnotism. She stated this despite the fact that over twenty other people in the room saw and touched the materializations and held conversations with them.

These kinds of cases, reported by Greene, fit in more with the idea that in these instances the spirit of the deceased person was actually appearing to the living. In her book *Apparitions*, she related the following two stories:

One November afternoon I had arrived home from school, and passing through the dining room I noticed my grandfather in his sitting room talking to my grandmother who had been ill. She was in her nightgown and robe. I entered the room and said hello to them, and told my grandmother it was nice to see her feeling up to being out of bed. After a minute or two of polite conversation, I said I had better go do my homework. My grandmother then said, "Barbara, it would be best if you didn't tell anyone I was up and that you spoke with me."

I went on upstairs and as I entered my own room it suddenly came over me that my grandmother was dead. She had died a month earlier.

And another case:

My husband died in August 1970. The following Christmas I spent with my married daughter. On December 27th we were all playing Monopoly and at the time I was not even thinking of my husband. I looked up from my game and my husband was sitting on the settee opposite. This I could not believe. I covered my eyes with my hands and looked again; he was still there. I must have looked very distressed, as everyone looked up from the game and enquired what was wrong. I was a little incoherent and wept, and my husband got up from the settee, crossed the room and went out, turning at the last moment, putting his head back inside the door and smiling at me. He appeared as in life, wearing his charcoal coloured trousers and open necked white shirt. I was overcome with grief and went to bed at once.

All these kinds of ghostly phenomena point to the fact that there are many things which we do not understand about how the universe works. The next time someone says to me, "You look as if you've seen a ghost," perhaps I have.

Chapter Nine

The Ghost in the Machine

The resistance to new ideas increases by the square of their importance
Russell's Law

The Electronic Voice Phenomena, better known as EVP, has been around a long time. I have experimented with it on many occasions. While living in London I obtained an unusual EVP while walking down a street with a friend, holding a hand-held recorder. My friend stated that he would like to hear the voice of his grandfather who had recently died, and the response, which came almost immediately, was "He is not here".

While I find the Electronic Voice Phenomena interesting, there are many unanswered questions surrounding it. Why are the phrases so short? Why are some of the statements meaningless? Unfortunately the EVP phenomenon has been the target of a number of zany religious groups who have labelled the communications as those coming from "demons" or "Satan". In over forty years of psychical research I have found no evidence of either one, but I have found plenty of evidence of the damage done by organized religion!

Professor Archie Roy, in a public address, asked the question, "Why can't they (the spirits) get it right? They have had seventy years to play with it. Still there is no method of having long, extended two-way communications via the electronic method. It is always promises, promises."

Archibald Edminston Roy BSc PhD FRAS FRSE FBIS, who died on 27 December 2012, aged 88, was Professor Emeritus of Astronomy and honorary senior research fellow in the department of physics and astronomy at the University of

Glasgow.

Archie was born in Clydebank, West Dunbartonshire. He joined the SPR in 1973, served as President during 1992-1995, and afterwards was elected a Vice President. He founded the Scottish Society for Psychical Research in 1987 and served as its President. He was a frequent contributor to SPR publications and conferences, and also appeared regularly on BBC Scotland television and radio programmes discussing his many interests.

A prolific author, he produced twenty books, including six novels, in addition to many scientific papers and articles. His books on psychical research include *A Sense of Something Strange* and *The Archives of the Mind*. He was awarded the Myers Memorial Medal by the SPR in recognition of his outstanding contributions to psychical research in 2004.

The EVP has progressed from humble beginnings to what it is today: ghost box recordings, visual recordings on computers and television and even telephones.

The first breakthrough came in 1956, when two psychical researchers, Attila von Szalay and Raymond Bayless (later the author of *Phone Calls from the Dead*) recorded on tape some extra voices that should not logically have been there. Although the voices did not speak very long (only a few words) or say anything of great importance, both Bayless and von Szalay knew they were on to something.

Then, in the summer of 1959, halfway across the world, a Swedish film producer, Friedrich Jurgenson, came up with some extra voices while trying to capture birdsongs on a tape recorder in the countryside. In the midst of the birdsongs he heard a faint human voice, a male voice speaking Norwegian, saying something about bird voices of the night. At first he thought they were stray radio signals. After replaying the tapes many times, Jurgenson recognized the voice of his mother, who had died four years earlier, saying in German, "Friedel, my little Friedel, can you hear me?"

Jurgenson continued his experiments and published the results in 1964. His book was read by Dr Konstantine Raudive, a psychologist in Germany, who began his own experiments. After three months he achieved results. By the time he published his first book on his work, in 1968, he had recorded some 70,000 word phrases. He also learned that if he tuned his radio to the so-called white noise between stations, the tapes recorded at those wavelengths would contain voices. Alex Schneider, a Swiss physicist, helped Raudive to develop a new method of recording to detect voices not heard by the human ear at the time of the recording but which could be clearly heard when the tape was played back.

In 1971 Raudive's book was published in English under the title *Breakthrough: An Amazing Experiment in Electronic Communication with the Dead*. When Colin Smythe brought out the English edition and began experimenting with the voices, he came up with the voice of the dead mother of Peter Bander, an associate publisher. Raudive recorded 72,000 of these voices on tape, of which 25,000 have been identified:

> The voice phenomenon offers the means to break through the confines of purely physical existence, for it has breached the material barriers surrounding our world. Death is not final, so the voices assure us; it is but a transition to a new state of being, and the impressions we received from the voice entities allow us a glimpse of that farther shore to which all must cross through death.

In recent years there have been paranormal phone calls to living EVP researchers from Raudive. George Meek, Sarah Estep and Mark Macy all received such calls. In the call Raudive stated, "This is the first bridge we have built to the States."

Raudive was by means the only person to have had long success with EVP. A parish priest in Switzerland, Father Leo

Schmidt, has recorded over one thousand of these voices. His results were published in his book, *When the Dead Speak*, in 1976, shortly after his death. One thing that makes this sort of phenomenon less than earth-shattering is the content. The voices say nothing dramatic, don't talk for very long, and perhaps the most important of all, are almost twice the speed of normal human speech.

I made a series of experiments myself in 1990, shortly after my book came out about life after death. The results were something less than spectacular.

Many earlier experimenters shared the same fate as myself. In 1921 F.R. Melton, a British inventor, published an article in *Light*, the magazine of the College of Psychic Studies, to the effect that he had invented a psychic telephone over which he had received voices directly from the dead.

Upon further investigation, it was discovered that some measure of psychic ability was necessary to operate the instrument, which actually was little more than a twenty-three inch long aluminium tube, three inches in diameter at one end and eight at the other, in which were placed a receiver and amplifier. A headset was attached to the output of the receiver.

Meanwhile, the same sort of instrument was being developed in the United States by a man called Francis Grierson. Few people, including his biographers knew that besides being an important literary figure, he was also a psychic and a medium who gave many demonstrations in Europe under the name Jesse Shepard. After his retirement, Grierson invented some sort of telephonic device over which he apparently received several post-mortem communications. These are described in a short book, *Psychophone Messages*, which he privately published in Los Angeles in 1921. Grierson lived out the rest of his life in Southern California and died there in 1927.

In 1947 a Dutch scientist named Zwann came up with what he called a spirit radio. Zwann claimed that he had received the plans for the device through mediumistic communications. According to several sources in September 1957, he achieved considerable success with it. However, no public demonstrations or reports were ever made or issued. Like so many would-be inventors, Zwann disappeared from the psychic scene as quickly as he had entered it.

A device similar to the Melton telephone also surfaced during the 1940s. It was developed by Harry Gardner and his associate, J. Gilbert Wright, a General Electric researcher. Gardner was a Spiritualist who believed he had developed an instrument that could amplify spirit voices. Wright died in 1959, and his spirit device has long been forgotten.

Sarah Estep, who died in 2008, was an American pioneer in recording the voices, starting in the 1970s. While I was living in Maryland I visited her and she explained how it all started:

When I was six years old, I became a complete unbeliever in life after death. That happened when my paternal grandmother died and my grandfather married another woman who with her son owned a funeral home. Each time my parents and I visited I would slip into the viewing room, when no one was around, softly close the door behind me and creep over to the casket. Standing on tiptoes, my hand on the casket edge, I'd look down into the face of the dead person about two feet away. There was no fear because I knew from my first view, the dead were dead and could never hurt anyone. I became convinced the only place a dead person went was into a hole in the ground; that death was a casket.

Living with the dreadful knowledge that most life only lasted sixty to seventy years, I could never completely enjoy what most young people do, as they become adults. I read non-fiction books during all spare moments, especially those that dealt with what we call paranormal, hoping to open the possibility within me, that life might not end. None convinced me. I liked the Seth books the most since they came closer to telling me ... you live forever.

Looking around further for something that would interest me at the library, I found *Handbook of PSI Discoveries* by Sheila Ostrander and Lynn Schroeder. There were two chapters about recording voices of the dead. They listed well-known people such as Harold Sherman and Walter Uphoff who thought that it might be possible to record voices of spirits.

I decided to try taping even though I didn't think I'd get a thing. I'd make 5-minute recordings every morning and evening, which the book recommended, and always asked the same questions. Then I'd play it back and there was nothing. On the morning of the sixth day, I was so bored I was ready to quit, but I'd determined to do it for seven days. I had the thought if anyone from spirit was listening to me, they must be as bored as I was, so I changed my questions and asked, "Please tell me what your world is like." Within 5 seconds a clear, Class A voice replied, "Beauty". My joy knew no bounds, however, I kept wondering if it was just my imagination that "beauty" was there even though I listened to it often. I played it for the rest of my family who were amazed. At dinner I said I wasn't going to stop taping but would continue with it each day. The others accepted this since they knew I'd received, "beauty".

At the beginning I'd go for weeks without a single thing. Again, I'd be ready to quit, but the invisible must have know that for they'd clearly come through and say, "Don't give up," or "Keep it up," so I did. After six months, they came through almost every morning and evening. I'd write in my log what was received, the question(s) I'd asked, their reply (if there was one) and grade the message: A, B, or C. Class A voices could be easily heard without headphones. I'd been told I should ask for a 'helper' so that's what I did.

Eventually a male voice came through and said his name

was "Styhe", my helper. He was with me for over 10 years. One time he sounded different, in that he spoke slowly and his voice was weak. I asked what was wrong and he said that he was tired. I knew then I had tired him by constantly asking him to help. I told Styhe I wouldn't call on him for a week, and so I didn't. At the end of a week I called on him and asked how he felt. In a loud, clear Class A voice, which was like his previous voice he replied, "I feel much better now for you!" It is possible to tire those on the other side if we continually ask them to speak and help us. One of the things Styhe did for me was often to bring to my morning recording the person I'd asked him to bring when I signed off the day before.

Many years have passed. I've heard from both parents, my husband, many friends and unknown individuals who come a time or two to speak. I've recorded messages in French and German (languages of which I have no knowledge). I'd write them in my notebook and then got the language dictionary from the library and often found the word I'd recorded and they'd make sense. Konstantin Raudive came through many times the first year, always Class A. He spoke English but one time I asked him to speak German so I could be sure I was hearing from him. He did, and I found that in the German dictionary. Raudive has also called me on the phone upon several occasions. The last time he called it was about my husband who had been at the hospital the day before. What he said about him here and when he passed on was very moving. I sent a copy of it to Ernst Senkowski, who listened to it, and replied that he was sure it was genuine. He had never heard anything like it and felt the same way I did.

Another contact I had for years and totalled over 100 messages with was a Class A male voice who said he was Jeffrey, and he'd been my brother in the 1700s in Philadelphia, USA. That could have been true. A grandfather (many times back) James Wilson moved here from Scotland in the 1700s.

He settled in Philadelphia and had 4 children. Jeffrey told me he was a 'lamp-lighter', which according to the encyclopaedia was started in Philadelphia at that time. Once I asked Jeffrey what he was doing now, and he replied Class A, "I'm trying to find the person that killed you." That was a shock. In my next recording I told Jeffrey, I appreciated what he was trying to do for me, but that was no longer necessary. I said it was wonderful hearing from him so often, but I felt he should move on further into spirit, and I hoped he would meet me, when I arrived there. I think (hope) he took my suggestion for I haven't heard from him since.

Another important American pioneer was George Meek. I did quite a bit of writing for George after he moved from Florida to North Carolina. George was an industrial engineer turned psychical researcher. In 1971 he began experiments in a Philadelphia laboratory to establish two-way communication with the dead. As I remember George, he was passionately devoted to the cause of exploring the subject of life after death and two-way electronic communication; George's device was dubbed "Spiricom" and has been the subject of much discussion both pro and con. George's approach differed significantly with the EVP researchers in that he wanted first to get in touch with discarnate scientists on the other side in order to obtain the information to make the device. "Hopefully the equipment we could jointly design would eliminate the need for a psychic or medium," George told me. "We want to use a practical engineering approach because there was no practical theoretical base to work from."

George assembled an impressive group of collaborators, intelligent men who had their feet firmly planted on the ground. One was Melvyn Sutley, Chief Administrator of the Willis Eye Hospital, and one of the founders of the Spiritual Frontiers Fellowship. Other members of Meek's research team were Paul

Jones, a physicist and electronic engineer, Hans Heckman, a computer specialist for Conrail in Philadelphia, and an electronics expert.

It was Sutley who launched the project on its way, when he learned through a medium that a deceased friend of his wanted to work with qualified engineers to develop a two-way communication device. The friend turned out to be none other than Francis Gray Swann who had been a professor of physics at Yale. Swann had died in 1962. During his life he had held many conversations about life after death. Before he died he told Sutley that he was convinced that there were "interspersed planes of existence beyond our physical awareness".

Swann began to provide the group with reams of technical information on how to go about establishing communication electronically. But he was not alone. Swann stated that he had brought with him several others who were able to help put the pieces of the puzzle together. Two well-known radio pioneers, Reginald Fessenden and Lee de Forest, were reported by Swann to have joined the team.

The research group was told that any sort of electronic communication with the "dead" would be impossible without the co-operation of people on the other side. As Swann put it, "The active application of the energies must come from us."

George's equipment was far more complex than that used by either Rauduive or Jurgenson. It consisted of a 300 megahertz generator, an antenna and a radio signal generator. Swann, still communicating through the medium, was encouraging: "The problem is to put the energies we work with together to produce the voice sound. As our work is done mainly through thought or mind energies, there can be the combination of certain energies to create voice."

George steered his course towards finding a medium to work with who also had an electronics background. By combining the two, George hoped to achieve what he had failed to do before:

to establish a link with a deceased communicator who could provide the details for a device that could successfully reproduce a voice, thus enabling two-way communication to take place.

George found him, in the form of Bill O'Neil, in the spring of 1973. After briefing him on the work of the Philadelphia research group, George explained in detail the electronic approach they were using. Bill told George that he thought that the radio might create a "mediumless" way to hear voices from the other side, at last proving survival after death.

Bill had a mediumistic gift that he neither understood nor trusted, a gift that had been with him since childhood. He welcomed the organized approach to working with his gift that George seemed to offer. His only question was, "How can I help?"

He received his answer almost two years later. Late one January night in 1975 he had an encounter with a deceased communicator who would help him put many of the pieces of the puzzle together.

He was sitting in his upstairs lab surrounded by a maze of electronic instruments, generators and radio equipment. Suddenly, as he glanced toward a darkened corner of the room, he noticed the head and face of a man, along with his right shoulder and arm. All Bill could manage to say was, "My God, who are you?"

He was shocked when the surprise caller answered, "They call me Doc Nick. I was a ham radio operator, too. What are your call letters?"

Doc Nick told Bill that he used to be a doctor. He also told him he would guide him along with further suggestions as time went by. Then, as mysteriously as he had come, he disappeared.

Four months later, Bill was to have another, similar encounter. But this time it was a different communicator who had come to pay a visit. Late in April of the same year a man who identified himself as William Kincaid materialized in Bill's lab. He told

Bill that he had worked for a food and grain store in Natchez, Mississippi while on earth.

"What I am here for is to assure you that there is no such thing as death," the man continued. "I want you to realize that death is just a word spoken by the ignorant to describe that part of existence that is on a different plane. Remember that! There simply is no such thing as death. Fear and ignorance about the transition from here to there is the one fact standing in the way of your knowledge and understanding of all things. On the present level, and on other planes of existence."

Baffled, Bill asked for more, but before he could get a reply the figure was gone.

Spontaneous visits from Doc Nick continued throughout 1975 and 1976, but still there had been no voice communication established through the electronic equipment. In the early autumn of 1976, Doc Nick had this to say about communication:

Spontaneous materializations are more likely to occur between those who are incarnate and discarnate when brought about by a common love for one another, husband and wife, mother and child, etc. This is not to say such communication cannot be accomplished if approached in a sincere, prayerful and loving manner, unlike the fraud perpetrated by 90 per cent of all mediums. Genuine spirit communication can and will be accomplished when science and religion eliminate the mystery that has involved the subject for thousands of years. Emphasis must be placed on the reality of natural, rather than unnatural aspects of the multiple planes of existence.

When will science and religion eliminate the mystery? This is not likely for several reasons. Once the mystery is eliminated the Church has no more power, and the Church will not give up that power. The Church controls people through fear. Fear of death and what comes after death. They are not likely to saw off the limb on which they are perched!

By July 1977, Bill had still been unable to record on tape anything his frequent visitor said. George's hopes had all been placed on electronic communication. What Bill desperately wanted was to capture Doc Nick's actual voice on tape, so that he could show George and the world that what he was hearing was valid, hard evidence for life beyond the grave.

Late one July evening, as Bill's mood grew worse, he encountered another mysterious visitor. It was a man, someone he had never seen before, tall and distinguished looking in a suit and tie.

"I need your help to carry out research in several areas," said the man.

"What kind of research?" asked Bill.

"Research in just the kind of thing you are doing right now, and not succeeding. I can help you."

The man identified himself as George Jeffries Mueller. He gave Bill his Social Security number and furnished him with information on his academic background, including naming many facts that could be checked out. He said that he had received a degree in physics from Cornell in 1930 and had also attended the University of Wisconsin. Mueller concluded his ghostly chat with a bit of information that was simply too specialized to be accidental if it checked out: "I once worked for the government and the United States Signal Corps. In design and development. A lot of miscellaneous electronic equipment, and a lot of specialized medical electronics for hospital use."

George started the wheels turning to check out the details of Mueller's earthly life. He found that Mueller had been enrolled in the University of Wisconsin when he said he was, in the class of 1928. A friend of George's, Walter Uphoff, confirmed that Mueller's record at Cornell was exactly as reported. George also found that the social security number was correct, a fact that appeared in no public data about Mueller. Also, a letter to Mueller's widow, whose address had been provided by the Social Security office, confirmed that Mueller had died on May 32, 1967.

Bill continued his chats with his friends from the other side, alternately with Doc Nick and Mueller. According to Mueller, the "white noise" used by the EVP researchers was no good to act as a carrier wave for the discarnate voices. Mueller suggested, instead, setting up a sustained background of thirteen varied tones, utilizing a stable DC power supply.

The breakthrough occurred on the night of October 21, 1977. As Bill adjusted the dials and frequencies of his equipment, a voice appeared, robot-like, but it was still a voice. Bill asked it to repeat itself. The moment they had been waiting for occurred. What followed was the first two-way communication with a discarnate being via electronic means:

Bill: Try it again.

Mueller: All right. Do you hear me now, Bill?

Bill: Yeah, but you make it sound just like … a robot.

Mueller: You hear … you hear, Bill?

The entire conversation lasted less than two minutes, but it was a beginning. It was the breakthrough that George and scores of other researchers had been hoping for. But who would believe it? As time went on, more and more conversations were recorded.

The SPIRICOM sounded a bit like somebody was talking through a Jew's Harp. The conversations recorded covered all sorts of topics from SPIRICOM improvements to magazine articles that Mueller's ghost read as they lay around the lab. Here's a sample of the conversations held between the ghostly Mueller and Bill O'Neill:

Doc Mueller: I think that the problem is an impedance mismatch in that third transistor.

Bill O'Neil: Third transistor.

Doc Mueller: Yes, the one that follows the input.

Bill O'Neil: I don't understand.

Doc Mueller: The preamp, the preamp.

Bill O'Neil: Oh, the preamp.

Doc Mueller: Yes, I think that, uh, we can correct that by introducing a 150-ohm, 100-half-watt resistor in parallel with a .0047 microfarad ceramic capacitor. I think we can overcome that impedance mismatch.

Bill O'Neil: Oh boy, I'll have to get the schematic ...

Here's another sample, it's a bit sillier:

Bill O'Neil: Yeah, I just turned on the tape recorder, Doctor.

Doc Mueller: Very well, William.

Bill O'Neil: (a bit angrily) You said to hurry back, and I did. That has been exactly one week ago.

Doc Mueller: Ho, ho.

Bill O'Neil: Yes, ho ho yourself. Cold weather has left us, temporarily anyway. It's raining. It's nice and warm. Of course you never know what to expect. I am going to try to put in a little garden this year.

Doc Mueller: Oh, wonderful. (pause) Send me a couple of carrots.

Bill O'Neil: What's that again?

Doc Mueller: A couple of carrots.

Bill O'Neil: Oh, carrots!

Doc Mueller: Yes, William, and a nice head of lettuce.

Bill O'Neil: A nice head of lettuce. I am not going to plant acres, Doctor. What's that? I think you were talking at the same time I was.

Doc Mueller: Well, perhaps. I said if somebody had some cabbage, I like fried cabbage. Oh, I love fried cabbage.

Bill O'Neil: Fried cabbage. Well, I like sauerkraut.

Doc Mueller: Well, you know what sauerkraut can do ...?

Bill O'Neil: Yes, I do. You know, Doctor, I never thought I'd see the day when I could, uh, talk to someone like you in the way we are doing, and if ten years ago someone had told me this was possible, I would recommend that they be sent to the 'funny farm'.

Doc Mueller: Well, perhaps you are right.

According to George: "SPIRICOM requires an operator with a very special type of psychic energy, and even such a person cannot consistently communicate."

Eventually Mueller stopped coming through. Before he left, he told O'Neill and George that he wouldn't be here forever. Within a month he was gone – but others came through – lots of others.

In mid-1978 all contact with the entity calling himself Doc Nick seemed to cease abruptly, both clairaudiently and through the electronic equipment. In his place Bill felt that Mueller's presence was making itself felt more and more.

About this time Mueller began giving Bill predictions about world events. One of them, in early October 1978, was startling. Bill was told that by a year from that date some new type of archaeological find would be made in Africa that would surpass all others to date. And in December 1978 Mueller gave another prediction that was fulfilled five weeks later. He said that within three months the Shah of Iran would be deposed. This occurred on January 16, 1979. Dr. Mueller had a much better track record of timing with predictions than any psychic I have ever consulted, most of whom get it wrong every time.

With the passing of over one year since the initial breakthrough, with no further communications, George grew concerned. Then in November 1979 part of Bill's house burned to the ground. Another setback. But despite this and other difficulties, Bill remained positive. He had begun receiving information early in 1980, clairaudiently from Dr Mueller, as to how to proceed with the device by beating different frequencies against each other.

In March 1980 Mueller continued with his predictions for the future. All American oil personnel would be banished from Libya in the very near future. This prediction was fulfilled in

November 1981, when Libya took over the American-run oil fields and most of the American oil companies sent their people home.

Ensuing conversations between Bill and Mueller were sporadic, to say the least. But, all in all, over thirty hours of conversation were logged over the device with Dr Mueller. The following extract from one of their conversations revealed that apparently Mueller was not much aware of life after death before his passing:

The most important thing ... the one benefit that you will find as the result of our contacts – you are aware! I was not aware of this side. I didn't know the potential over here before. So, when I got over here, it was like waking up in the morning and not knowing where you are. Like having a bad dream.

In one of their last conversations Mueller pointed to the temporary condition which foreshadowed the end of their contacts.

"Williammmmmm," Mueller's voice echoed through the equipment.

"Yes sir?" Bill answered.

"I cannot be here forever. I cannot guarantee how long I'll be visiting here. However, I will do my best. Do you understand, William?"

"Yes, sir," Bill replied.

"There is a time and a place for everything. So, as I have mentioned before, this is something I think you should be aware of."

Not long after that, all contact with Dr Mueller ceased.

Hanna Buschbeck, another EVP researcher commented that the work George had done should be accepted by any open-minded person.

Before her death, Buschbeck worked extensively in the field of paranormal research, and organized international meetings with other prominent researchers to discuss experimental parapsychology. She died at the age of 78.

Buschbeck wasn't the only one to welcome George's breakthrough. Alex MacRae, the Scottish electronics engineer who worked on the Skylab project, has spent years conducting his own EVP research. In a letter to George, MacRae had this to say:

> Paranormal voices are real and it is only the inability to absorb this admittedly incredible fact that has held up progress for so long. EVP will bring the strongest evidence. The tangible existence of this evidence will be a thorn in the side of Russia, where it has been reported that they have done their own experiments. They may have to rewrite their philosophy to include EVP, and maybe we will see things in a different perspective.

Since no tape recording of the life voice of Dr Mueller exists, it is impossible to prove whether the voice sounds enough like him to be identifiable. But on numerous occasions people who have conducted EVP research have found voices that were clearly identifiable.

Peter Bander is one of those people. In the preface to Konstantine Raudive's book *Breakthrough,* he describes his experience of clearly recognizing his own mother's voice:

> I was just about to give up when suddenly I heard this rhythm. I played it again, and once more. It is very difficult for me to narrate clearly what happened next; suddenly I heard a voice – quite distant but very clear. I played this part of the tape again because I was absolutely sure that I had fallen a victim of my own imagination. The voice was, if anything, clearer. A woman's voice said in German: "Mach die Tur mal auf," "Why don't you open the door?"... As soon as I heard the voice I recognized the speaker; although the voice spoke terribly fast and in a strange

rhythm, I had heard it many times before. For eleven years before her death I had conducted my entire correspondence with my mother by tape, and I would recognize her voice anywhere. This was my mother's voice.

Later that evening, I went back to the tape recorder and played that tape over and over again. There was no doubt about the voice being on that tape.

EVP, George's Spiricom device and the early spirit radios or telephones all seem to point to the idea that somehow, by a process which we are perhaps soon to discover, discarnates are able to transform their thoughts into electromagnetic waves that reach us as sound. There seems to be little difference whether the mechanism used is a tape recorder or a telephone.

There have been many phone calls from the dead. In their book *Phone Calls from the Dead*, D. Scott Rogo and Raymond Bayless turned up dozens of such cases. Rogo writes,

> Back in 1976, out of pure curiosity, Raymond Bayless and I began collecting, investigating, and tracing phone calls from the dead cases. We wanted to see if these types of psychic phone calls were worth studying seriously. And what we did discover came as quite a shock. Hundreds of people have received this type of phone call from the dead or other types of phantom phone calls.

One interesting case involved a young jazz singer in his mid-twenties who had apparently received such a phone call from his deceased grandmother. Rogo and Bayless interviewed Karl (the young man) and his friend Peter, who had been a witness to the incident:

> When I was a little kid my grandmother was about eighty per cent deaf. We had a phone with an amplifier on it so that she could amplify whatever was coming through, but it still

didn't help very much. Up until the time I was sixteen or seventeen I would give her a list of numbers and tell her where I was going. If she needed me for an emergency or something, she would call any place I went. She'd merely dial the number. She wouldn't know if it rang or if anyone answered. She would keep repeating over and over again, maybe four to six times, "This is Karl's grandmother, would you please send him home, I need him." It was a regular occurrence for me; it happened all the time. The last phone call like that I might have gotten at anyone's house was when I was, maybe, sixteen.

In 1969, two years after his grandmother's death, Karl and his friend Peter DÁllesio were talking together in Peter's basement when the upstairs phone rang.

Peter remembers the incident well. "We were talking or playing or something, and I heard my mother, not arguing – I don't recall any words – but I know my mother's tone of voice, and she was getting a bit miffed." They didn't pay much attention until Peter's mother yelled down to Karl, "There's an old woman on the phone. She says she's your grandmother and she says she needs you. She just keeps saying it over and over again."

"When I grabbed the phone no one was on the line," Karl recalled.

One opinion that seems to be going around concerning the phantom phone call and the EVP in general is that the voices are "demonic" in origin and are here to "mislead us". It is my view that there is not any misleading going on, it is the Church that is doing the misleading.

But in every age there are members of the clergy who are far-sighted enough to know that, given the opportunity, psychical research and religion could work hand in hand. One such person was Monsignor Charles Pfler, a chaplain to the Catholic Holy

See. He says,

> It is a reality backed by experience and established by evidence open to all, that the dead live and can communicate with us. It has been established beyond all doubt that these voices are clearly audible to everyone.
>
> Only the most narrow minded rationalism would want to banish all mystery from our lives. The reality of the universe in all its aspects consists on a visible and invisible realm and we have a long way to go yet before we can grasp the implications of the physical, visible part alone.
>
> Theology should not create too many difficulties for Dr Raudive's discovery, for dogma is being looked at with fresh eyes today, and quit fundamental articles of faith are under review, so that it is surely reasonable to accept for consideration this new evidence concerned with the nature of life hereafter, upon which, one must not forget, Christian theology is very vague.

Chapter Ten

The Foreseeable Future

I've heard a lot of psychics bring up the term "free-will," in their readings. It's usually inserted as a disclaimer after the predictions are made. Should you get a psychic reading from me, you will not hear such a disclaimer ... because I don't believe in free-will.

I cannot emphasis enough that I do not have empirical evidence to support my claims. All I have is my 17 years of experience of communicating with Spirit and studying the movements of the heavens to draw my conclusions.

Psychic Abbeygale Quinn
www.michiganpsychicmedium.com

God watches over the cosmic life of the group-souls. And, according to their growth, He plans or designs the future of the life of mankind. But because it was all imaged by Him at the beginning so is there little to change in the vast cosmic picture that lies in His imagination.

F.W.H. Myers, *The Road to Immortality* by Geraldine Cummins

The prediction of the future by psychics, mediums and clairvoyants has always fascinated me. In my astrology readings I was always able to predict to a certain degree, but the most amazing predictions I have come across are those made by mediums and psychics. But how can anyone predict the future if we can go out and change it all by free will? I have looked more closely at this area of the paranormal than any other. Are we free or bound?

A posthumous communication from the famous psychical research Frederick William Henry Myers tells us that it was all imaged at the beginning by God and that we have little free will to change. This would seem to account for Rudyard Kipling's dream about being in Westminster Abbey that came true in every detail. Kipling referred to it as being shown a slice of the reel of his "life film".

Myers communicated through automatic writer Geraldine Cummins in several books. In *The Road to Immortality* he wrote:

THE term "free will" presents different meanings to different people. For some it implies the idea that in all we do we are following out our own particular fancy or desire so far as is possible. For others, free will seems to imply simply the right to choose, the right, when we come to cross roads, to follow the particular lane that seems, from our point of view, the most alluring.

Perhaps we decided to travel along the beech-shaded road and not the road that is open on every side. Who makes that decision? I should call it the aggregation defined by the term, body, soul, and spirit. Now, all these are built up out of various elements, but all are one creation. They have been slowly shaped through the ages. All the hereditary influences must be included. All the influences of a psychic and a spiritual character are there. These seem innumerable to our finite minds. Circumstances, friends, enemies, relations, all help to mould that inner being which makes the decision to follow that beech-shaded road. Does it not strike you, therefore, that you are asking what is impossible because of the very nature of our being when you make the demand that free will must rule? We are obviously merely the creation of many other men and women living and dead. Therefore we are largely the victims of their varying influences and are bound to follow those tendencies implanted in us.

In other words all mankind is, in a sense, one, and yet many. Man's history, his character since the dawn of the world, might be conceived as a vast web ever growing and growing, and the source of it all is to be found in the Master Spinner who is responsible for every particle of that fine fabric, for the whole history, the whole character of man since the beginning of time.

Now, you must realize that as God is the Creator, the Great Master Builder, He knows what shape the life of the individual will take before that individual is born. He knows exactly the nature of the unborn babe, how he will develop from the hour he leaves his mother's womb, where his tendencies will lead him, the manner in which circumstances will mould him. For the great picture of all creation has been conceived in the imagination of God before ever the babe has evolved out of what we call the void. For instance, the future of the earth is imaged already in the imagination of God. It has happened because He has already thought it. But what has not happened is the change in the individual soul, the manner, for instance, in which it reacts to the trials and the joys of life. The reactions of the soul are all that matter in connection with your earth life. Will sorrow embitter you? Will ruin but nerve you to fresh effort? In the latter instance, you create within yourself in that you increase the power of your will, increase your courage. Or will you give up hope and sink into penury, thus increasing the weakness of your character? You have, in short, free will only in the sense of creation, only in the moulding of your own soul. Now that is the important and vital factor in connection with your earth life.

As difficult as this concept is for people to grasp, I have accepted this as the true one for many reasons. It accords with my experiences as an astrologer, making predictions with a definite timing. It accords with my experiences of going to mediums and clairvoyants who read for me and in which the predictions came true, sometimes with accurate timing.

Think of Creation this way. Everything that is going to occur has already occurred. Your life, others, the events in the Universe, they have already happened, we just haven't arrived there yet. Creation is as a giant movie reel. The Creator has already made everything and all the events that are to occur. Each of our lives is in the reel. The reel runs at a set speed (time frames). What will happen in your life, say next year, is already on the reel, you just haven't arrived at that point yet. Call it destiny or whatever. The Creator can look backward or forward in the reel as HE pleases. HE can stop the reel if so desired. Our lives, from birth till death are already fully contained within the reel. The reel runs at the set speed (time) of the universe, as far as we are concerned. Everything you do throughout every moment of every day is already contained within the reel of life. Everything.

One of the most dramatic of my experiences in connection with having a future prediction come true took place in the summer of 2003. I was living as a helper and caretaker for an elderly lady in London. One early autumn, I was giving an astrology reading to a young woman client. At the end of her reading she pulled out some small Tarot cards and proceeded to lay them out. "Let me read for you," she said.

The woman proceeded to tell me that one year from that date I would no longer be living in that house. Something would occur, she said, that would force me to leave. I thought this prediction very unlikely. I was friends with the lady who owned the house and could see no reason why I would leave. I quickly forgot the prediction and went on with my life. Then in the early summer of 2004 Wendy, who owned the house, told me that she planned to transfer ownership of the house to her two daughters in order to avoid death duties tax upon her death. She assured me that nothing would change with regard to my living there.

In August 2004 I went to see a clairvoyant in the Belgravia area of London. She told me that I would be returning to the United States in November. "You will have to go back," she told me, "but not at the beginning of November. It will be the third week of November."

Then in September, just prior to the transfer of the ownership of the house to the two daughters, one of the daughters informed me that she planned to rent out my room at a high cost and I would have to leave. The predictions were fulfilled in every respect, right down to the timing. I was unable to get a flight at the beginning of November and ended up returning to the USA the third week of November.

How can such things happen if there is free will? My friend Alex Tanous told me the following stories about some of the predictions he has made in the past:

I told the priest he was going to break his foot. He scoffed at the prediction. But three weeks later I saw him with his foot in a cast.

One of my confessions in this period was to a young Marist priest, Rev Arthur Duhmel, S.M, whom I greatly admired. It was not a happy experience. I knew that he intended to go to Guadalcanal shortly. As I talked to him, another premonition came over me, "Don't go overseas," I told him. "If you do, you'll never see America again. You'll be killed, bayoneted through the throat. And your church will be burned to the ground."

He took my warning gravely, but with no comment. And he left as scheduled. On October 14, 1942, he was bayoneted through the throat and killed, along with two nuns. The three of them were buried near the remains of the church which was burned to the ground.

Alex had seen a slice of the priests "Life film". Alex remembers some of the predictions he made during his early years, all which came true with uncanny accuracy:

One day, not long after I got out of the service, I was sitting in the family living room when a woman visitor asked my mother for a reading. Mother took out the cards, as my father had done years earlier. She was about to start the reading when another thought occurred to her.

"No," she said. "I'm going to let my son do this reading." She handed me the cards. Now I'd had many psychic experiences in my life and I'd many times watched my father give readings. But I'd never done one of my own.

I told the woman to cut the deck into three parts and pick out several cards. To this day, I don't know why I did it this way. I do know that the cards had absolutely no significance. The message came to me when I took the woman's hand. It was a vision of her husband's death.

Reluctantly I told her what I saw: that within ten days, her husband would die. As I said these words, he wasn't even sick, so far as anyone knew. Ten days later, my prediction had been borne out, to my sorrow.

And this one, also from Alex Tanous:

Bob Ridge, of Portland, Maine, asked me about his upcoming insurance exam. I'll let him describe what I said:

"I asked Dr Tanous: when I take my insurance exam, will it be in Portland or Augusta, how many questions will it have, will it be subjective or multiple choice, and what will my mark be? His reply was that I would take the exam in Augusta, there will be 100 questions and it will be multiple choice, and you'll get an 87."

"Sure enough it was in Augusta, 100 questions, multiple choice, and I got an 88."

And this one:

For the first time in my life, I also began to make predictions in public, to groups of people. It was at this time I said Robert Kennedy would never be President – he would be shot. I also predicted that Richard Nixon would be nominated for the presidency, though he hadn't yet announced his candidacy. I foretold the death of the U.S. astronauts in a non-space accident and my prediction was borne out. I predicted that a vote to admit Red China to the United Nations would fail, which it did. I said that a petition to remove Governor Ronald Reagan of California would be circulated, and it was. I said a Negro named Marshall would be appointed to the Supreme Court long before anyone had mentioned Thurgood Marshall for the post.

The uncanny thing about predicting the future is that often the predictions happen against all odds. One of the strangest experiences I ever had was when I received a reading from a psychic in Virginia Beach in 1982. I had applied for the position of music director at a classical music format radio station in northern Michigan. I told the psychic that I hoped I got the job because it would be the first time in my life in which I would hold a management position, and not just an announcer's job. The psychic told me that I need not bother to go. That I would get the job and leave in exactly seven months. I dismissed the prediction as sheer rubbish.

I was hired in July 1982. By January of the following year I was in dispute with the radio station management over a large sum of money. A special fund had been set up by National Public Radio to allow independent producers on their own time to go out and record interviews with writers, artists and musicians and to make them into short segments that could be distributed nationally via satellite. The scheme was called the Satellite Programme Development Fund. By the end of 1982, I had written and produced twelve of these segments which were uplinked via satellite from WHA in nearby Madison, Wisconsin. The Fund accordingly paid me over one thousand dollars for this work. In January I was asked by the radio station management to turn over the money to the radio station because, even though I had produced the segments on my own time, they claimed the money was rightly theirs because I had used their equipment to produce the segments. I refused to part with the money and quit the job. How could the psychic in Virginia Beach know this would happen?

In the winter of 1986, while living in a cottage in Woodstock, Vermont, I travelled to California to do research on a book. I consulted psychic Vicki Johnson, then of Laguna Beach, California. She told me, "March of next year will be the major turning point in your life. One thing I see right around that time is you are going to get on a plane and go to a foreign country. I feel that you will live out the rest of your life in a foreign country."

Well it was not March of "next year". It was March of 2014! In March 2014 I moved to Spain. She was off by 25 years.

Another experience in my life of psychic prediction took place in early 2005, not long after I returned to California from London as the psychic had accurately predicted. Having lost my home in London, I was not doing well financially. I was looking for a live-in job. I had a phone reading with British medium Honor Church, a Spiritualist. She told me that I would be moving to the San Francisco Bay area from southern California where I was at the time and that I would be living in a large home owned by a man whose initial was "R".

"You will be ok with this job," she told me. You will have to leave the man who you are helping out with some food in the microwave, where all he has to do is push a button, you will be ok."

I went to live in a house owned by a man named Rick. Rick claimed he had a serious chronic back problem despite the fact that doctors could find nothing wrong with him, Rick lay on the floor all day and only got up for a few brief moments to eat meals which it was my job to prepare. The routine we established was that I would leave soup in the microwave which Rick would warm up.

Impressed with the accuracy of these predictions, I booked three more readings with Honor Church over the next year and a half. In the next reading she told me about a woman that I was going to meet very soon. Whenever I hear that something is going to happen soon I roll my eyes to the ceiling because invariably the time frames are wrong. I am reminded of the prediction George Woods got about meeting Betty Greene via the mediumship of Leslie Flint. "Very soon," he was told, "a woman will come and join you in this work." It happened seven years later.

"This woman will teach you to breathe properly," Honor Church told me. "It could be something like Hatha yoga." She then proceeded to describe the sort of house this woman lives in. "You could put my whole house into one of the rooms in this woman's house," Honor said. "The house is huge," she told me, "and it has its own swimming pool. Near the house is a very large tower with lights on it at night. It could be a radio or TV tower or mobile phone tower but it is visible from where this woman lives."

"You are going on a cruise with this woman," she went on, "but you're not paying for it. She is. One cruise you go on the ship is the size of New York City. Wait until you see the car she comes driving up in. Very fancy. Once you meet her, sweetheart, you will never have to worry about money again."

I recorded everything she said and waited one year. Nothing happened. The following year I got two more readings. In those readings she told me the woman had a dog and that the gardens would be out of this world. "There is something about deer that are tame enough to come near her home."

Fascinating. Seven years later it still hadn't happened. Then, in the early part of June 2014, I went with a friend, Christine Wessel, to the tiny village of Mijas Pueblo to see a clairvoyant, Mark Bajerski. Mark held court in the basement of a tiny New Age bookstore. Half English and half Polish, Mark had clients coming from all over Europe for readings. As I settled into my chair that day, Mark poured some oil onto my hands and asked me to remain quiet.

He began to speak about my mother who had passed away in 1993. "Your mother wants you to know she is sorry for what she did to you. She was manipulated."

When my father died, my mother married a man who was no good and he turned my mother against me.

I had come hoping to hear something about a TV series I was planning but instead Mark turned the reading in a much different direction.

"Within two years from now you are going to be in the arms of this woman whom you have not met yet," Mark said. "This woman lives here in Spain and this is where you will stay."

Here we go again, I thought.

"And if she wants to share her wealth with you, I think you should take it."

I nearly fell off the chair. "Did I hear the word wealth?" I asked.

"Yes, this woman is quite wealthy," Mark replied.

I left not knowing what to think. Honor Church's similar predictions were now over eight years old. Perhaps I should just forget it.

Then, in April 2015 I went to see Mark again for another reading. He had moved his office to the basement of a golf hotel. Once again, he rubbed oil on my palms and told me to relax.

"You still have much work to do," he began. "You are a lighthouse, a beacon. You have lived a life that is more interesting than most people's. A life that holds great wisdom that needs to be shared with the world. Start writing. Writing is the doorway that leads you to where you are going. Make sure you get the title right. Spiritually you are connected to a higher vibration. The book will be taken to from four to seven countries."

"The sea is important," he continued. "I see two dogs walking. There is a woman at the side of you, each has one dog. You are walking on the beach holding somebody's hand. She is not in your life yet. You will have love, help and guidance from her, not just a caring ear.

"Look down at her feet when you meet her and see what kind of shoes she has on, they are going to be stilettos with a designer logo, they are designer shoes. This woman doesn't eat burgers. She comes from old money and she is used to good things. Gary, you have the gift to make a woman laugh. She has long hair, and her eyes are not brown so they must be either blue or green. She has a tiny birthmark. She is a princess – self-made!

"This woman has two living children, and one in the Spirit World. Her husband was very wealthy. The money came from a company connected to gas and oil. She could be an American lady or else has some connection to America in some way. I get the number ten, or ten months from now, Gary. That would put it a February 2016. From May to May the clouds are disappearing and there is a new beginning. This woman has more than one house. The most important connection with her for you is that she needs to trust and believe in somebody who will take time for her."

I am still waiting for these events which have been predicted by Mark Bajerski to occur.

I began by stating my feeling that in some way we cannot understand, these events have already happened. How, otherwise, could the clairvoyant possible predict such details with uncanny accuracy?

The late Dorothy Allison, already mentioned in a previous chapter, was able to predict the exact date events would happen in the future. In the following case, in which a banker disappeared from a commuter train on his way home from work, Dorothy was able to describe the events surrounding the discovery of the man's body, the date, and the details including a prediction about the people who it turned out found the body, even though those people had only decided that very morning to go to the location for some archery practice.

Dorothy described an arrow which was not far from an old row of tyres, scattered in a line on the ground. She could make out the numbers "166" in the far distance, and then, in a different way, the numbers "222" appeared.

"Look for the numbers one, six, six and two, two, two around the body. They don't have anything to do with each other, and they might not be places," she warned him, and then added, "I see a playground too."

The detective, a man named Lupo, looked puzzled.

"I see that arrow and archer again," Dorothy said.

"What do you suppose archery has to do with John DeMarrs?" Lupos asked.

"I can't tell. There might be an archery range nearby, or maybe he was killed accidentally by a flying Indian with a bow and arrow. You'd be a horse's ass if you had written that down," Dorothy laughed.

"I see the playground, tyres, two guys, and a place that looks like a plant or factory that has burned down."

"What the hell are two guys in a playground supposed to tell me," Lupo asked.

"I didn't say there were two guys in a playground. I don't know either."

By late January, Lupo and Dorothy had travelled back and forth along the riverbanks in the vicinity of several train stops. Dorothy began to feel that searching any more was futile. Then the numbers "222" came to her again and she told Lupo that he should hold onto those numbers. They would be important.

That night Dorothy called Lupo at home and told him that Demars would be found on Febrary 22. She decided that was the meaning of the numbers.

It was on February 22 that the police learned that a body had been found in the Passaic River. A wallet had been found on the body, with the identification inside.

Lupo drove the several miles to the site of the body as he had been told. He discovered that the body had been found behind a Two Guys department store. Here was the Two Guys department store, there the playground, and as he stood there, he saw the charred ruins of what had been a paint factory across the river. The number "166" was painted on a tugboat that was tied up under the bridge.

Lupo could see the tracks made by the coroner and all the policemen in the mud. He followed the tracks through to the park where a teenage boy watched him approach.

"Do you know how they found this guy?" Lupo asked.

"Yeah, me and my dad found him. We were shooting arrows at a target and one got away. I ran to chase it down by the river's edge, and I saw that man's leg in the mud and plants. I ran back and my dad went over to Two Guys and called the police."

The father and son archery team had not decided until that very morning to go shoot arrows down by the river and yet Dorothy Allison had been able to predict that they would several months before. How?

Many people believe totally and absolutely that the future is not fixed. One rather ridiculous New Age idea is something called creative visualization. It simply means you can change the future by visualization. But what happens when it doesn't work?

New Ager Remez Sasson writes,

Almost every day, I receive mail from people, asking why they are not getting results from creative visualization.

People get excited when they come to know about the wonders visualization can do. They begin to visualize enthusiastically, hoping to get quick results. Sometimes, they do get results quickly, but then, this power seems to stop working, or to bring only minor results.

Why does this happen?

If visualization produces results once or more times, why doesn't it do so always?

There must be an explanation.

Yes, there is an explanation. The explanation is that creative visualization is a lot of nonsense.

Let us say for the sake of argument that there is a chance that the future is not totally fixed. If that were so, it would not be possible to predict who would show up on any given night for a lecture because each person's free will would determine whether or not they attended. And it certainly would not possible for a psychic to predict who would sit in a certain seat weeks and even months before the event. And yet that is exactly what happened with psychic Gerard Croiset and the famous "chair tests".

The best way to describe them is to give an example. The aim is to prove precognition and Croiset successfully performed hundreds of these tests before witnesses in various European countries. On 6th January, 1957, in front of witnesses at the University in Utrecht, Croiset was handed a seating plan for a meeting to be held twenty-five days later in The Hague, fifty-eight kilometres away. The guest list had not yet been made up, but there were thirty chairs in the seating plan and Croiset chose chair number nine. Asked who would be sitting in that chair on the night, Croiset handled the chart then began talking into a tape recorder with his impressions. He said that a cheerful, active, middle-aged woman would sit in chair number nine and she was interested in caring for children. He said that between 1928 and 1930 she used to walk between the Kurhaus and

Strassburger's Circus in Scheveningen. He claimed that, when she was a little girl, she had many experiences where there was cheese-making. He saw a farm on fire and some animals burned to death.

He mentioned three boys, one with a job overseas in a British territory. He alleged she had been looking at a picture of a Maharajah. He wondered if she experienced a strong emotion about the opera 'Falstaff' and thought it may be the first opera she'd ever seen. He also stated that on the day the meeting took place she would take a little girl to the dentist and this visit would create a lot of commotion.

All together there were twelve detailed statements. I've only mentioned seven, but they were all transcribed and sealed into an envelope. The following day the host was told she could go ahead and issue thirty invitations. On the night of the meeting, the participants were given a copy of Croiset's statements and asked to check if any applied to them, and a procedure was used with random cards to ensure that they did not sit in a chair of their own choice, and that they did sit in the seat randomly allocated to them. Only after this had been carried out did Croiset enter the building, thus precluding his influence upon the process of seat selection. The woman in seat number nine was asked if any statements applied to her and she agreed that many of them did. Virtually none of the statements applied to the other twenty-nine people. Later the woman in seat number nine was interviewed and the accuracy of Croiset's statements was deemed to be remarkable.

She was active, vivacious and forty-two years old, with an interest in child care. When her father came home on leave from abroad he took her walking in Scheveningen near where Croiset had outlined. As a child she often visited farms producing butter and cheese. Once, on a farm, she witnessed a horse killed by lightning and was profoundly affected by it. This was not quite the same as Croiset's statement of her seeing animals burned in a fire. She had a brother-in-law, one of three boys who was in Singapore, a British territory, during the war. A few days before the meeting she had seen a picture of a yogi and had had a conversation with her son about it. This seemed the nearest fit to Croiset's reference to a Maharajah. And with regard to the opera 'Falstaff', it was the first opera she had sung as a professional opera singer and she had fallen in love with the tenor in it. With regard to the visit to the dentists, she had taken her little daughter on that very day to deal with a cavity. The child had been frightened and had suffered pain during the visit.

If free will exists then it is sure and certain that it would be impossible for a clairvoyant to see in advance which chair a person would sit in when they came to attend a lecture. Croiset repeated this test hundreds of times, sometimes with Professor Bender selecting the chair, sometimes with Croiset selecting the chair and anywhere from two days to two months ahead of the event. Although I have had the pleasure of meeting many famous psychics and clairvoyants, I was unfortunate that I never met Croiset.

In the summer of 1990, my friend Alex Tanous died. I was on Madeline Island, off the coast of Wisconsin writing a book and restoring an old historic garden for some people who had a summer home there on the shores of Lake Superior. I received a call from Alex's brother that he had died. I was heartbroken.

It was around this time that I met Jess Stearn. Jess's book, *The Sleeping Prophet* had made him famous in metaphysical circles. The book was the story of Edgar Cayce of Virginia Beach, where I was born. I bumped into Jess in the A.R.E. library. We were both writers, and my book *A Life Beyond Death* had just come out. Jess began telling me about a psychic he knew by the name of Maya Perez. Jess was in a restaurant when he was approached by Perez.

"How about a reading, big boy?" The pungent invitation came from a darkish woman sitting at a table off to the side –

words that were to change the course of his life forever.

"What kind of a reading?" he inquired.

"Oh, about your past, present and future."

"You must be a fortune teller."

"No, I'm a sensitive," she replied.

As he turned to go out, she called after him, "Well, I can understand your being upset and all, because you've just gone through a divorce. But you have two lovely children to show for it, haven't you? The boy is the older, the girl is the younger?"

"Yes, that's true," Jess said, looking around to see if anyone was nearby, feeding her information.

"You're thinking of marrying somebody, but you're never going to see her again."

By this time, Jess was intrigued enough to sit down with the woman, who turned out to be psychic Maya Perez.

"She described everything that was going to happen to me in the next thirty years," Jess admitted in retrospect. "She told me my son would go into the law. He went into the N.Y. Police Department and was head of an anti-crime movement. She told me my daughter was going to go into healing. She's a doctor now up in Wyoming. They weren't even teenagers at the time. She told me I was going to get married in eight or nine years to a golden-haired blonde, which happened."

The psychic went on to describe how Jess would become involved in 'this field'.

"What field?" inquired Jess

"My field."

"What kind of field is that?"

"The metaphysical field." "You're going to write about me."

As she continued the reading, Maya Perez made some very definite predictions about the reporter's future, things which he couldn't have possibly known at the time. She mentioned, for instance, that Jess' third book would be a bestseller which would subsequently take him out of the newspaper business.

His eighth book, she foretold, would become a bestseller which would be sold all over the world.

All of these predictions came about with startling accuracy. As foretold, Jess detailed his incident with Maya Perez in his first book, *The Door to the Future*. His third book, *The Sixth Man* quickly became a bestseller, established his career as an author, and took him out of the newspaper business. *Edgar Cayce: The Sleeping Prophet*, his eighth and most well-known book, is still being sold all over the world today.

"I had no way of knowing at that time that all these things were going to happen," Jess observes, "but it did make me very much aware of something I had not even known existed before – this metaphysical world, this world of the occult. I had heard enough to make me realize as a reporter that there was something here tangible. She [Maya Perez] keyed in very tangibly on the [then] present situation, the things I knew about."

The incident with Maya Perez and other subsequent experiences involving psychism had made a profound impact upon the young newspaperman, so much so that they became a formative influence in his life.

"People that I talked to at that time sensed an openness about me that wasn't there before."

Not long after that, Jess invited me to his home in Malibu, California. Through Jess I met actress Susan Strasberg. While having lunch one day in Hollywood, Susan began to tell me about her friendship with Marilyn Monroe.

"Marilyn did not commit suicide, she was murdered," Susan told me. "She was murdered because she was going to hold a press conference and tell the world about the false promises that were made to her by Bobby Kennedy and his brother. The Kennedy's couldn't have that, so they had her killed."

Susan was very interested in the psychic and went on to tell me about many readings she had received through contacts made by Jess Stearn. Susan always wanted to live in Italy but sadly she died before she could make that happen.

Aside from Gerard Croiset, there were two other psychics who were also from Holland who achieved recognition for being able to accurately predict the future. Why there should be three psychics, all from Holland who became famous for this skill I do not know. Maybe there is something in the water.

The second psychic was Peter Hurkos. Hurkos's psychic abilities manifested from a head injury caused by a fall from a ladder when he was 30 years old. The parapsychologist Andrija Puharich was impressed by the stories about Hurkos and invited him to the USA in 1956 to investigate his alleged psychic abilities. Hurkos was studied at Puharich's Glen Cove, Maine, medical research laboratory under what Dr. Puharich considered to be controlled conditions. The results convinced Puharich that Hurkos had genuine psychic abilities.

The third psychic was Marius B. Dykshoorn. To my way of thinking, Dykshoorn's predictions were the most amazing of all. I only heard about him toward the end of his career when he was living in New York and I could not afford to go and see him for a reading.

Dykshoorn recalled some of his most famous predictions in his book *My Passport Says Clairvoyant*. Dykshoorn openly states:

> I believe in predestination, and I am convinced that if I have a definite psychic impression that something will happen, it will happen and cannot be avoided. Neither I nor any of the people involved can intervene to prevent its occurrence. If I see that a person will have an automobile accident, for example, then he will have it even if he resolves never to drive again. One day he will get the urge to drive, and then it will happen.

Dykshoorn recalls a case in which he tried to prove that there is free will:

Only once that I can remember have I tried to intervene to prevent something happening that I had seen through my gift. In mid-1971 in Charlotte, North Carolina, a woman told me her son had entered an air race. I told her that she must try to talk him out of it. "Tell him he must not go in it," I said. But I knew that he would and be killed. I knew that when his mother told him I had said he must drop out of the race, he would laugh and he would enter anyway.

It all happened. The woman told her son not to enter, but he laughed. He entered the race, crashed and was killed. Perhaps I should never have tried to intervene. I knew that it was the boy's destiny that he die in that crash, but I hated to see it. I believe in predestination, and believe it was my destiny that I should learn about it beforehand, and in the woman's, that she should learn about it from me.

The following prediction is also intriguing because in it Mr Dykshoorn was able to predict who the new tenants of an apartment would be even before the existing tenants had moved out. Shirlee Sharatz of Charlotte, North Carolina wrote the following testimony:

If you will recall, on August 6th you told me that the lease from my apartment would be broken and we would be leaving Charlotte shortly.

September 1, we were evicted and left Charlotte on October 24th. You also predicted that three girls would take over the apartment and that they would be nurses. You have been absolutely right.

The day I moved, I saw the maintenance man and he told me three girls were moving into my apartment and I asked him were they nurses? And he said he didn't know for sure, but they worked at Charlotte Memorial Hospital. I wrote to a neighbour and asked her to find out what those girls are and the reply came yesterday – nurses.

It sure softened the blow when I got evicted to know that this was supposed to be happening.

And this one, which was written up in a sworn statement notarized by a notary public in the state of Florida.

STATE OF FLORIDA

COUNTY OF DADE

Before me this day personally appeared ALEX S. MARCHANDO, who, being duly sworn, deposes and says that on November 11, 1971, he consulted with MR M.B. DYKSHOORN. MR MARCHANDO told MR DYKSHOORN he planned to visit his 91-year-old mother in Youngstown, Ohio over the coming Thanksgiving holidays. MR DYKSHOORN said it would be better if you could go over the Christmas holidays; "You would see more relatives and could have a nice visit with your mother before she dies, because she will only live a week to ten days after Christmas."

MR MARCHARNDO changed plans and visited his mother and many relatives over Christmas. He returned to Miami December 29th and before midnight January 3, 1972, his brother telephoned informing him that his mother had just died.

Sworn to me and subscribed before me this first day of February, A.D 1972 Monty F. McFarland, Notary Public.

And this one, from Australia. Part of this reading reminds of the chair tests done by Croiset when he would describe the future occupant of a chair:

Several years ago I was the proprietor and owner of a restaurant in Sydney. At this time I met Mr M.B. Dykshoorn, who to my surprise told me that my restaurant would be burnt out not once but twice. I forgot about the prediction until two and a half years later when my business was in fact burnt out. Still I thought this may have been coincidence, but eight months later the building was burnt out again.

On a different occasion Mr Dykshoorn visited a restaurant of which I was the owner and told me that the following day the chair in which he was sitting would be occupied by my first employer. I doubted this for two reasons: firstly because that particular place was occupied every day by a regular customer; secondly because my first job had been at a hotel in Holland when I was thirteen years old and I could not even remember the name of my employer at the time.

The following day my regular customer brought a guest to lunch, although he sat in his usual place. Then suddenly the two men changed places so that the guest occupied the chair Mr Dykshoor had nominated. I was later introduced to the guest, who, after learning my name, said he had been the manager of the hotel in Amsterdam when I had worked there.

And this one, which comes from New South Wales:

You said my marriage would be broken and I would remarry a man I already knew who would have to do with the sea, would have three children and his work would have to do with the Crown. All this would transpire during a period of four years and I would change my name during the tenth month. Subsequently I did remarry a man I had known for ten years with the name Seabrook which brought in the sea and his business was importing which brought him under the wing of the Crown as most of his business was involved with Her Majesty's Customs with the crown over the door. Our wedding date was the 6th of October (10th month) before the four years stipulated by you had expired. You also predicted I would assist my husband with my hands to make money and now I have successfully started a manufacturing section in which my hands are in use creating. You also said I would go overseas (which I did). My husband prior to my second marriage was the manager of a substantial retail business which you said I would leave and a male would take over, which did happen. I had been in this position for twelve years and with no intention of leaving.

This final prediction made by Dykshoorn serves to illustrate my point that free will plays no part in what happens in a person's future. Dykshoorn predicted his client would work in a building that did not exist at the time of the reading. This bares some similarity to the dream of Christine Mylius who dreamed of her acting parts in films, the scripts of which had not even been written yet:

Mr Dykshoorn told me that I would work for a large company in a circular building in Sydney, although at the time I was entirely self-employed and had no intention of changing that situation. Mr Dykshoorn further told me the nature of the catering work I would supervise in my future employment.

I now manage a catering business in the circular tower in Sydney known as the Australia Square Tower. The nature of my work is almost exactly as Mr Dykshoorn described. It is remarkable that at the time Mr Dykshoorn made his prediction, the Australia Square project had not been commenced or even conceived yet.

Comedian Jack Benny once quipped, "Everything good that happened to me happened by accident. I was not filled with ambition nor fired by a drive toward a clear-cut goal. I never knew exactly where I was going."

But are there any accidents? The following account was quoted by psychical researcher Gustave Geley in his book, *Clairvoyance and Materialization*. It concerns the tragic end of a young actress, Mademoiselle Irene Muza. Muza was in a hypnotic trance when she was asked if she could see what awaited her personally in the future. She saw the following: "My career will be short. I dare not say what my end will be: it will be terrible."

Naturally the experimenters, who were greatly impressed by the prediction, erased what had been written down before awakening Mlle. Muza from the trance. She therefore had no conscious knowledge of what she had predicted for herself. But even if she had known, it would not have caused the type of death she suffered.

It was some months later that the prediction was fulfilled. Her hairdresser allowed some drops of an antiseptic lotion made of mineral essences to fall on a lighted stove. Mlle. Muza was instantly enveloped in flames, her hair and clothing were set on fire and she suffered burns so severe that she died in the hospital a few hours later.

The most bizarre story of seeing the future took place in an aeroplane. I believe the Creator's "imaged future" is allowed a sneak preview on rare occasions, perhaps when the wind is blowing in the right direction.

Sir Victor Goddard knows what I'm talking about, because in 1935 he had his own bizarre experience over an airfield in Drem, Scotland.

One day that year, he was flying to Edinburgh from Andover, England. And while on this perfectly ordinary flight, he passed over a dilapidated airfield in Drem, Scotland. This place had long been abandoned, to the point where foliage had overtaken most of the area and cattle had made themselves at home. That's what Goddard saw as he flew over – a farm, with a whole lot of nothing going on.

So he continued on his way, until he reached his destination at Edinburgh.

A few days later, Goddard began his trip back to Andover. He took the same route, which would lead him once again over Drem, but before he could get there, he ran into a peculiar storm. I call it peculiar, because along with high winds and torrential rain, the storm clouds were yellow. It didn't take long for Goddard to become disoriented and lose control of his plane.

He tried to regain control by climbing above the yellow clouds, but they seemed to have no end. His plane began to fall. Fortunately for him, that's when something unexpected happened: the clouds broke, and he could see the ground again.

Off in the distance was the Drem airfield.

As he approached the airfield, hoping to reorient himself, suddenly the storm vanished and the sky turned bright and sunny. It stopped raining. Everything became clear. But something was different, this time.

The airfield at Drem was no longer abandoned. In fact, it looked good as new. He could see mechanics down below, and four planes, each painted yellow, sat on the runway.

One was a model he'd never seen before, a monoplane unlike anything in the Royal Air Force in 1935. And what were the mechanics wearing? Blue overalls? This, along with the yellow planes, Goddard found strangest of all – RAF mechanics in 1935 wore brown overalls, not blue, and there were no yellow planes, to his knowledge.

Goddard didn't have much time to think about it, though, because he was flying too quickly to truly understand what he was seeing. By the time he'd passed over the airfield, the storm had suddenly returned, and the bright sunshine dissolved into hard rain and those strange yellow clouds engulfed him once more. Once again, he found himself battling for control of his aeroplane. But this time he won, and was able to land safely at his home base.

When he finally landed, he couldn't help but tell his friends what had happened. As you'd expect, he was met with scepticism, and afterward he mostly kept the story to himself. He didn't want anyone to think he was crazy, after all. He'd later retell it (among other things) in his 1975 book *Flight Towards Reality*.

The final twist to this bizarre account? In 1939, the vision that

Sir Victor Goddard saw at the Drem airfield actually came to pass. The RAF began to paint their training planes yellow, and a new monoplane, the Magister, just like the one he witnessed in 1935, joined the roster. By that year, even the mechanics' overalls had been updated to blue. And, of course, the airfield at Drem had made a comeback.

Let us consider the account of the fate of the giant airship R-101 which, in 1930, left Cardigan at 7 p.m. on Saturday October 5 for India, and crashed on a hill near Beauvais, France at 2:05 a.m. killing all forty-six on board.

Medium Eileen Garrett, who taught and studied at the College of Psychic Studies in London where I was lucky enough to be able to study in 2000 and 2001, had several distinct and specific precognitions of the R-101 disaster, and talked about it in her memoir *Many Voices*, published shortly before her death:

The perceptions that I receive are clear-cut and distinct, like the unrolling of a film or spool. This is what living can be likened to: a continual unwinding of the thread from the spool – a current of feeling moving in space in the continuity of progress and unity of action ...

The loss in 1930 of the airship known to me as the R-101 had been "seen" by me three times in a period of five years. The first appearance of the phantom airship occurred in Hyde Park. I had taken my terrier to the Serpentine to swim. I looked above, and there was a silver ship moving easily in the direction of the west. It made no conscious impression on me then. I had no relationship with anyone who might be flying. It was simply there in the sky. There was no confusion, and it flew above me slowly to vanish into the sunset.

I saw the same object again two years later. I was in the neighbourhood of Holland Park en route to the College of Psychic Studies. It was about 2 p.m. A high wind was blowing fleecy clouds across the sky. Out of a bank of clouds I saw an airship. It wobbled, then dipped. Puffs of smoke blew out and hid the undercarriage. Then the clouds covered it.

When I left the College I bought the late papers, expecting to read of the disaster. But there was nothing on the front pages, nor was there anything next day. This time I was confused. I had actually seen smoke, even as I had seen it happen during the 1916 raids. Through that week I watched the daily papers, but once again there was no account to be found.

I again saw the airship overhead in 1929, and again smoke merged from the great envelope. I remember standing still frozen to the spot. White puffs caught the rays of the sun, then turned into a dense cloud. Again the clouds obscured the smoking ship. This time I was deeply upset. I knew this was serious. That it wasn't happening was unthinkable – but again there was no report.

After three such phantom happenings, it was hard to convince myself there had been no airship. Yet no one could explain it. There had been no known airship disaster anywhere. I often wondered why such visions happened to one so completely disinterested as it was.

Of all my experiences with psychic phenomena, precognition is the most baffling. How can anything be predicted before it happens? There are many accounts of near-death experiencers who were told of future events by deceased relatives during their NDE experience. This would somehow postulate the theory that the dead can see the future. If we grant the non-physical existence of human beings, it is a short step to assuming that more advanced spirits exist with greater powers of seeing ahead than have human beings.

But merely to say that spirits know the future is only to push the real problem of precognition further back. If they do know the future, how do they know it? If the answer is that for spirits time does not exist and that they see events as present which for us are in the future, then I repeat my question: what is the status of the events when spirits see them in *their* present? So we are back where we started, and postulating the existence of spirits has not helped us to understand the problem of precognition.

I am drawn toward the idea put forward by Frederick Myers which I stated at the beginning of this chapter, namely that the Creator imaged it all at the beginning. If we could imagine some pattern of Cosmic unfolding as existing – say, God's plan for the world – then we might suppose that some spirits could have access to this plan, or at least to some portion of it, and this may account for how mediums and clairvoyants access their information.

If all the events of a lifetime coexist, past, present and future being one and a whole, of which the consciousness is not wholly aware, then we may come close to an understanding of precognition. This would easily account for Croiset's prophetic chairs and the London psychic who told me that I would have to move out, a year before it happened. If the future already exists, if one's path is neatly tracked, a glimpse of the future becomes more intelligible. You may then ask if the future is ordained, why trouble to make decisions? Why assert yourself? Why bother with conflict, conscience, obligations, duties, development? Why swim against the all-powerful tide? The answer may lie in a thought which was given to me by clairvoyant Abbeygale Quinn:

Even if free-will is an illusion, our choices still matter. Everything we think and do is a necessary part of the divine manuscript that is Existence, including pondering imaginary possibilities. Our choices have profound effects on our lives, whether or not Somebody-Up-There already knows what those decisions will be.

I highly encourage you to live your life as though you have

free-will. It will enrich your experience in this incarnation, even if your decisions are ultimately already known.

However, if ever you look to the past with regret, remember this: the events of your life were written before the beginning of creation, and there's no other way things could have played out.

Chapter Eleven

Second Time Around

When I was a boy, the thought of heaven used to frighten me more than the thought of hell. I pictured heaven as a place where there would be perpetual Sundays with perpetual services, from which there would be no escape. It was a horrible nightmare. The conventional heaven, with its angels perpetually singing, nearly drove me mad in my youth and made me an atheist for ten years. My opinion is that we shall be reincarnated.
Prime Minister David Lloyd George

One of the most fascinating experiences I have ever had with regard to psychic phenomena was when I was regressed to a past life. This took place in Virginia Beach at the Edgar Cayce Foundation when I was twenty-three. Cayce's work reinforced the idea that each of us has lived before, many, many times. In the regression, I was told to go back to a time before I was born. As I moved back through time, I saw myself as a monk. This would be in direct contrast to my lifestyle now. And yet it was as clear as though I were living it.

The concept of reincarnation shocked and challenged Edgar Cayce and his family. They were deeply religious people, doing this work to help others because that's what their Christian faith taught. Reincarnation was not part of their reality. Yet, the healings and help continued to come. So, the Cayce family continued with the physical material, but cautiously reflected on the strange philosophical material. Ultimately, the Cayce's began to accept the ideas, though not as "reincarnation". Edgar Cayce preferred to call it, "The Continuity of Life." As a child, he began to read the Bible from front to back, and did so for every year of his life. He felt that it did contain much evidence that life, the true life in the Spirit, is continual.

Reincarnation is the belief that each of us goes through a series of lifetimes for the purpose of spiritual growth and soul development. The past merely provided a framework of potentials and probabilities and an individual's choices, actions, and free will in the present determines the actual experience lived this time around. Rather than being a fatalistic approach to life, it is much more one of nearly limitless opportunities. Within this framework of lessons that need to be learned as the soul strives to meet itself is the central idea that the soul is constantly experiencing the consequences of its previous choices. This concept is expressed in Biblical terminology as, "What you sow, you must reap" and is generally labelled "like attracts like" by students of reincarnation.

Another key idea from the readings is the idea of Karma. The word karma is a Sanskrit term that means "work, deed, or act"; it has also been interpreted to mean "cause and effect". Although the readings definitely agree with this concept, perhaps one of their most intriguing and unique philosophical contributions is the idea that karma can simply be defined as memory. It is a pool of information that the subconscious mind draws upon and can utilize in the present. It has elements that are positive as well as those which seem negative.

Reincarnation is a concept that encompasses not only Eastern thought but also all of the major religions of the world. It's a concept that can allow us to have more compassion, one for another. It's a way we can begin to look at all facets of life purposefully. However, it doesn't really matter if another individual believes or doubts the theory of rebirth. For some it can be a helpful concept; for others, confusing. The reason for believing in reincarnation is not so that we can dwell upon the past or brag about the possibility of having been someone famous in the past. The wisest student of reincarnation knows that we have all had incarnations in lowly and lofty circumstances.

Instead, the purpose is summed up in one of the Cayce readings:

> In the studies, then, know where ye are going ... to find that ye only lived, died and were buried under the cherry tree in Grandmother's garden does not make thee one whit better neighbour, citizen, mother or father! But to know that ye spoke unkindly and suffered for it and in the present may correct it by being righteous – that is worthwhile! (5753-2)

While some students of the Cayce readings suggest that we will always return to earth and incarnate again, and in fact cannot escape the "wheel of rebirth", I do not agree with this concept.

Evidence supplied by the over 500 direct-voice sittings with George Woods and Betty Greene recorded with medium Leslie Flint shows that many of the communicators were through with the earth life, with no need or intention to return again.

Of course, the very idea of reincarnation is a thorn in the side of many Spiritualist groups. But researchers in the second half of the twentieth century have established valid cases for reincarnation beyond all doubt. Anyone who is willing to spend a few hours in the library of the Society for Psychical Research, London, will eventually be forced to throw up his arms in surrender. The sheer volume of cases makes it nearly impossible to dismiss them as the work of a fanciful or over-active dream state.

One researcher who helped to turn the tide was Dr Ian Stevenson, a University of Virginia psychiatrist, whose book, *Twenty Cases Suggestive of Reincarnation* has become a classic, offering a fascinating insight into rebirth. Stevenson undertook the investigation of cases of children who at a very early age claimed to have memories of a previous existence. He took care to establish that the information which the children were able to provide about their purported former lives wasn't gleaned by normal means.

Some of the best information we have about the nature of reincarnation comes from the sittings that Eira Conacher had with her deceased husband through Leslie Flint in the 1960s.

Following the death of her husband in 1958, Mrs Conacher began having sittings with Flint. She recorded the sittings, in which her husband was the communicator during the years 1960 to 1967, and made them into a book, *Chapters of Experience*, in which Douglas Conacher delves deeply into the mystery of human incarnation and reincarnation.

Conacher repeatedly emphasizes the fact that human beings do not always incarnate again. He says,

> I think the most important thing to realize in regard to reincarnation is the fact that it is something which is not necessarily essential in every instance; in other words not everyone incarnates again, although many do – in fact, the vast majority. But, of course, we have to go back centuries upon centuries and realize that there are many souls who have incarnated on several occasions, and now do not feel the need to incarnate again.

Conacher was given the opportunity to view many of his earth lives, and he stressed throughout the talks that it is impossible to make judgements about the morality of a person's life in any given incarnation, because to some extent a person is the product of the age in which he lives. As he pointed out, there are things which simply don't happen in our lives today which were commonplace one hundred years ago. For instance, we no longer hang people for stealing a loaf of bread.

Conacher, like Cayce, stressed that we are the product of many experiences which we have gained over many lifetimes, and only after we have had innumerable experiences can we become fully-fledged individuals. Also like Cayce, Concacher stressed that, in accordance with the Divine Plan of the Creator, we choose the circumstances of our earth life:

> Particularly do we have to clarify this business of birth and how we are born, and, of course, why we are reborn. In the first instance we must understand that although we are individuals in a sense – that is we have built up certain characteristics and have separate personalities – we are fundamentally of the same spirit.
>
> When we feel the need, as one has done in the past, to return to earth, we have to decide or at least have some idea as to what would probably be the best environment in which to be born. For instance, if one felt that it was necessary to know poverty and suffering and struggle then one would obviously choose parents who were, by their very circumstances, impoverished. The physical body as such may not even have been brought into being, the seed possibly not even sown, when we decide.

One communicator who had some thoughts on reincarnation was Mike Fearon. In a sitting in 1963, Fearon spoke on the subject of the soul's eternal progression:

> We can see ourselves as we once were in a previous incarnation, not only on earth, but in a previous life or form of life on a previous stratum of being. In other words, once you can accept the fact that all life is a continuation, a step by step progression, and that on a different sphere or plane where once we were we have a realization of self living in that condition.
>
> We can see how we have made progress. It doesn't mean to say that we are more than one person. There are many facets, if you like, to an individual character or personality. We go from stage to stage, and condition to condition. We have the ability to tune in to the past. Not only our own past,

but the past of the world. We can see the world and tune into a particular period of history. Perhaps it might be a period of history in which we ourselves played some part. We can see in retrospect our lives as they once were. All this gives us an insight into the evolution and development, not only of ourselves, or the human race, but we learn wisdom and a strength is gained from that wisdom which enables us to visualize not only the present as we know it, but the future that is yet to come. There is no beginning and no end. Life is. It is a permanent thing. We are going through phases of knowledge and experience and existence, and as we move from one to another, so we gain more and more experience which makes us prepared for a new step or new venture further afield.

Although I cannot validate my past life regression experience, reincarnation seems to make sense. If reincarnation is a reality, let us hope we can gain the most of the life we are living now.

Chapter Twelve

Just One More Thing: What's It All About? Or "Brother Can You Spare a Paradigm?"

Just one more thing, sir. Just one more thing.
Lieutenant Columbo

What's it all about, Alfie?
Is it just for the moment we live?
What's it all about when you sort it out, Alfie?
Are we meant to take more than we give?
Burt Bacharach and Hal David

Cary Grant: I got into this by accident. What's your excuse?
Eva Marie Saint: It's the first time anybody's asked me to do anything worthwhile
North By Northwest, Alfred Hitchcock

What does it all mean? Is it possible to connect the dots and tie the subjects in the foregone chapters together? Could near-death experiences, visits from aliens, communications from mediums and prophecies of the future all be tied in together in some strange way we don't understand? In order to make sense of these experiences we must create new paradigms. More important, we must get rid of the old ones.

I have come to accept my forty years of experiences with psychic phenomena as normal. Although they are not everyday occurrences, they seem to fit into a larger picture, one that encompasses the meaning of life itself. My feeling, which I cannot prove here, is that life is a drama which plays itself out from lifetime to lifetime. We are the players in that drama.

The great psychical researcher F.W.H. Myers, writing through

Geraldine Cummins, seems to validate this idea in his concept of what he calls the Great Memory. Myers says:

> The Great Memory is, if you will, the subconscious mind of the whole human race. In our life, as in yours, there is the consciousness, the self, known to other discarnate beings who live in the same state as those akin to them fundamentally. But there is also a deeper self, which is the self of the world, imperishable as I believe, containing what was and is, containing also what shall be. For the history of man from the earliest to the latest times is all within what is sometimes called "The Tree of Memory". You may say, "But future events have not yet happened, so how can they have shaped themselves upon the ether?" I tell you they have happened, for they have already been born in the imagination of God. But the future is difficult to read, I mean difficult for men to read, because the memory of the future has not been so deeply impressed upon the invisible timeless substance, in that it has been thought only once and not twice, thought by the Maker of the Universes: therefore, it is very fine and faint, and only its echo is caught by certain mortals who have the inner hearing. Whereas the gross and clumsy subjective thinking of man causes past memories to be, from the point of view of the sensitive, more definitely shaped in the flowing energy.
>
> I want you to understand the significance of this vast memory in the lives of the ever-living, whom you may call "departed souls". These, in pursuing their present existence, can live away from the memory of all past existence, or they can resume a vanished personality by picking up the threads from the Great Memory and sucking in from them, as you might suck a sugar cane, the nourishment of a past personality. It is not always perfectly shaped when the discarnate being endeavours to communicate. Sometimes only a little of the

past individual's garment of mortality is taken from the great storehouse and, for a brief while, displayed. Now I would call your attention to an important point in this connection. We, you and I, are each recorded on some page in this Great Memory. We must, as players in a drama, re-learn the old part before we endeavour to speak to our friends on earth, through a medium. As a rule we neglect this task, or we succeed in obtaining only a glimpse of the memory that enshrines our vanished personality. We have vanished and we have not vanished. It is hard to explain this duality. Fundamentally we are the same as we were when a loved wife, mother, or sister bade us "good-bye" in the earth life. We are the same in the sense that we should continue to have a feeling of repulsion for certain things and people we disliked on earth, and the old affections would flame up if we met again those people and things that were dear to us. But if by personality you mean the sum total of our earth memories – our knowledge of Greek and Latin, our knowledge of concrete facts – then we are indeed changed, in that we can, as a rule, only resuscitate the old knowledge by obtaining contact with that part of the Great Memory which is ours. Yet we do retain – apart from it – our old mentality, much of its idiosyncrasies. That part of ourselves that is no longer integral, that has become detached, is the fleeting physical consciousness of that period when we bade the earth farewell; is the aggregation of memory concerning facts in our earth life, concerning certain concrete knowledge memorised by us. Emotional memory remains an integral part of the soul, for it comes from the creative Life.

What have my experiences with psychic phenomena taught me? That there will always be just one more thing. With each new revelation there are more questions. We are told that even those on the Other Side do not have all the answers. From my point of view, the problem is that very few people are interested in asking the questions. I cannot "prove" that Myers is right. I cannot "prove" that Carl Jung came to visit me at a materialization séance when I was sixteen years old. I cannot "prove" that several clairvoyants accurately predicted my future. But I feel that we are all on an endless journey, one with no beginning and no end. Unlike the beer commercial that says, "You only go around once so you have to grab all the gusto you can get." I feel we go around many times. The point is to get all that you can out of this experience. And, in doing that, you are fulfilling your destiny. You are standing at the door to the future. A future shaped by quantum physics. It is a future that spells the end of superstition, and religion, and religious beliefs. You are looking at the dawn of a new era. I will not live to see it but your children and grandchildren will live to see it. Exactly like the time when man discovered that the earth was round, we are about to emerge into a time of renaissance. Get ready for it.

About the Author

Gary Williams was born in Norfolk, Virginia in 1949. He entered radio as a profession after graduating high school. In late 1979 and early 1980, while working at world-class TV and radio Public Television station WGBH/Boston he began to have a series of psychic and paranormal experiences that led him to investigate the paranormal with an open mind that, while outside the framework of normal reality, these experiences may constitute a yet undiscovered reality. With the dawn of the 1990s, quantum and particle physics began to present a framework that could account for these experiences. After studying astrology with Isobel Hickey in Boston he had a major consciousness shift after an encounter with a Catholic priest who read past lives and revealed that the Church had hushed it up for centuries. Following this encounter he went on to develop his own psychic abilities and in 1989 met and became friends with psychic Alex Tanous, a Portland, Maine psychic who also taught parapsychology and did healing work. Their friendship lasted until Dr Tanous's death in July 1990 from cancer of the pancreas.

Following a series of what he describes as a "load of nonsense radio jobs" he turned his attention to acting at the turn of the century, landing the part of the psychic in the Paramount film, "Bruno" starring Sasha Baron Cohen. He wrote a book about life after death in 1989, *A Life Beyond Death*. He moved to Spain in 2013 and has set up a foundation to investigate paranormal claims outside the boundaries of normal physics.

His hobbies are gardening and classical music. He is unmarried.

The author can be contacted at gary@garywilliamsparanormal.com

I shall not commit the fashionable stupidity of regarding everything I cannot explain as a fraud.
Carl Jung

Knowledge is heading toward a non-mechanical reality. The Universe is beginning to look more like a great thought than a great machine.
Sir James Jeans

Let us so live that when we come to die, even the undertaker will be sorry.
Mark Twain

With thanks to:
The Society for Psychical Research
The American Society for Psychical Research
Stanton Friedman
Susan Strasberg
Mark Bajerski
Anne Mackinson
Guy Lyon Playfair
The Alex Tanous Foundation for Scientific Research
Norman Williams Library, Woodstock, Vermont
The Edgar Cayce Foundation
College of Psychic Studies, London
Leslie Flint
George Woods and Betty Greene
The National Film Board of Canada
Carl Jung

The author is grateful for permission to quote from copyrighted materials:

Journeys out of the Body by Robert Monroe, copyright 1971 by Robert A. Monroe. Reprinted by permission of Doubleday, a division of Bantam, Dell Publishing Group

Phone Calls From the Dead by D. Scott Rogo and Raymond Bayless, copyright 1979 by D. Scott Rogo and Raymond Bayless. Reprinted by permission of Prentice-Hall Inc.

Voices in the Dark by Leslie Flint, copyright 1971 by Doreen Montgomery and Leslie Flint. Reprinted by permission of Macmillion London Ltd.

No Goodbyes by Adela Rogers St Johns, copyright 1981 by Adela Rogers St Johns. Reprinted by permission of McGraw-Hill.

The Haunting of Hill House by Shirley Jackson, copyright 1959 by Shirley Jackson. Reprinted by permission of the Viking Press.

God Is Not Great by Christopher Hitchens. Copyright 2007 by Christopher Hitchens. Reprinted by permission of Atlantic Books.

BOOKS

ALL THINGS PARANORMAL

Investigations, explanations and deliberations on the paranormal, supernatural, explainable or unexplainable. 6th Books seeks to give answers while nourishing the soul: whether making use of the scientific model or anecdotal and fun, but always beautifully written. Titles cover everything within parapsychology: how to, lifestyles, alternative medicine, beliefs, myths and theories. If you have enjoyed this book, why not tell other readers by posting a review on your preferred book site? Recent bestsellers from 6th Books are:

The Afterlife Unveiled
What the Dead Are Telling us About Their World!
Stafford Betty
What happens after we die? Spirits speaking through mediums know, and they want us to know. This book unveils their world...
Paperback: 978-1-84694-496-3 ebook: 978-1-84694-926-5

Spirit Release
Sue Allen
A guide to psychic attack, curses, witchcraft, spirit attachment, possession, soul retrieval, haunting, deliverance, exorcism and more, as taught at the College of Psychic Studies.
Paperback: 978-1-84694-033-0 ebook: 978-1-84694-651-6

I'm Still With You
True Stories of Healing Grief Through Spirit Communication
Carole J. Obley
A series of after-death spirit communications which uplift, comfort
and heal, and show how love helps us grieve.
Paperback: 978-1-84694-107-8 ebook: 978-1-84694-639-4

Less Incomplete
A Guide to Experiencing the Human Condition Beyond the
Physical Body
Sandie Gustus
Based on 40 years of scientific research, this book is a dynamic
guide to understanding life beyond the physical body.
Paperback: 978-1-84694-351-5 ebook: 978-1-84694-892-3

Advanced Psychic Development
Becky Walsh
Learn how to practise as a professional, contemporary spiritual
medium.
Paperback: 978-1-84694-062-0 ebook: 978-1-78099-941-8

Astral Projection Made Easy
Overcoming the Fear of Death
Stephanie June Sorrell
From the popular Made Easy series, *Astral Projection Made Easy*
helps to eliminate the fear of death, through discussion of life be-
yond the physical body.
Paperback: 978-1-84694-611-0 ebook: 978-1-78099-225-9

The Miracle Workers Handbook
Seven Levels of Power and Manifestation of the Virgin Mary
Sherrie Dillard
Learn how to invoke the Virgin Mary's presence, communicate with her, receive her grace and miracles and become a miracle worker.
Paperback: 978-1-84694-920-3 ebook: 978-1-84694-921-0

Divine Guidance
The Answers You Need to Make Miracles
Stephanie J. King
Ask any question and the answer will be presented, like a direct line to higher realms... Divine Guidance helps you to regain control over your own journey through life.
Paperback: 978-1-78099-794-0 ebook: 978-1-78099-793-3

The End of Death
How Near-Death Experiences Prove the Afterlife
Admir Serrano
A compelling examination of the phenomena of Near-Death Experiences.
Paperback: 978-1-78279-233-8 ebook: 978-1-78279-232-1

The Psychic & Spiritual Awareness Manual
A Guide to DIY Enlightenment
Kevin West
Discover practical ways of empowering yourself by unlocking your psychic awareness, through the Spiritualist and New Age approach.
Paperback: 978-1-78279-397-7 ebook: 978-1-78279-396-0

An Angels' Guide to Working with the Power of Light
Laura Newbury
Discovering her ability to communicate with angels, Laura Newbury records her inspirational messages of guidance and answers to universal questions.
Paperback: 978-1-84694-908-1 ebook: 978-1-84694-909-8

The Audible Life Stream
Ancient Secret of Dying While Living
Alistair Conwell
The secret to unlocking your purpose in life is to solve the mystery of death, while still living.
Paperback: 978-1-84694-329-4 ebook: 978-1-78535-297-3

Beyond Photography
Encounters with Orbs, Angels and Mysterious Light Forms!
John Pickering, Katie Hall
Orbs have been appearing all over the world in recent years. This is the personal account of one couple's experience of this new phenomenon.
Paperback: 978-1-90504-790-1

Blissfully Dead
Life Lessons from the Other Side
Melita Harvey
The spirit of Janelle, a former actress, takes the reader on a fascinating and insightful journey from the mind to the heart.
Paperback: 978-1-78535-078-8 ebook: 978-1-78535-079-5

Does It Rain in Other Dimensions?
A True Story of Alien Encounters
Mike Oram
We have neighbors in the universe. This book describes one man's experience of communicating with other-dimensional and extra-terrestrial beings over a 50-year period.
Paperback: 978-1-84694-054-5

Dreamer
20 Years of Psychic Dreams and How They Changed My Life
Andrew Paquette
A ground-breaking, expectation-shattering psychic dream book unlike any other.
Paperback: 978-1-84694-502-1 ebook: 978-1-84694-728-5

Electronic Voices: Contact with Another Dimension?
Anabela Mourato Cardoso
Career diplomat and experimenter Dr Anabela Cardoso covers the latest research into Instrumental Transcommunication and Electronic Voice Phenomena.
Paperback: 978-1-84694-363-8

The Hidden Secrets of a Modern Seer
Cher Chevalier
An account of near death experiences, psychic battles between good and evil, multidimensional experiences and Demons and Angelic Helpers.
Paperback: 978-1-84694-307-2 ebook: 978-1-78099-058-3

Spiritwalking

The Definitive Guide to Living and Working with the Unseen
Poppy Palin
Drawing together the wild craft of the shamanic practitioner and
the wise counsel of the medium or psychic, Spiritwalking takes the
reader through a practical course in becoming an effective, em-
pathic spiritwalker.
Paperback: 978-1-84694-031-6

What Dwells Within

A Study of Spirit Attachment
Jayne Harris, Dan Weatherer
A book discussing the work of leading paranormal investigator
Jayne Harris and her studies into haunted objects.
Paperback: 978-1-78535-032-0 ebook: 978-1-78535-033-7

Readers of ebooks can buy or view any of these bestsellers by
clicking on the live link in the title. Most titles are published in
paperback and as an ebook. Paperbacks are available in traditional
bookshops. Both print and ebook formats are available online.
Find more titles and sign up to our readers' newsletter at
http://www.johnhuntpublishing.com/mind-body-spirit.
Follow us on Facebook at https://www.facebook.com/OBooks
and Twitter at https://twitter.com/obooks.